SIT STAY PRAY

Lina Speaks Again about Her
Life with a Difficult Momma

SIT STAY PRAY

Lina Speaks Again about Her Life with a Difficult Momma

THE SECOND TWO YEARS

Little Big Ears (a.k.a. Lina)

—Beaver's Pond Press—
Minneapolis, MN

Cover photos by Frank Steiger Photography

ISBN: 978-1-64343-909-9
Library of Congress Catalog Number: 2019906425
Printed in the United States of America
First Printing: 2019
23 22 21 20 19   5 4 3 2 1

 Beaver's Pond Press, Inc.
7108 Ohms Lane
Edina, MN 55439-2129

(952) 829-8818
www.BeaversPondPress.com

To order, visit www.ItascaBooks.com or call
1-800-901-3480 ext. 118. Reseller discounts available.

For dogs everywhere who, like me,
are busy caring for their humans.

CONTENTS

Forewoof ix

1. Flight to Florida 1

2. Tweeting: The New Bark? 7

3. Recovering: The Concussion and the Election 11

4. The Big Reveal 17

5. The Photo Shoot 19

6. More Fun in Naples 24

7. Even More Fun in Naples 29

8. The Usual Pre-Trip Drama 32

9. Scotland 35

10. The Last Straw 40

11. *Lina Unleashed* Released 48

12. Continuing Chaos 50

13. Yappy Hour 53

14. A Phone Call from Camp 57

15. Photo Shoot: The Sequel 59

16. The Annika Intercollegiate 65

17. The Book Club 68

18. Not Fake News 71

19. Perpetual Patient 73

20. Momma Works It 77

21. Christmas Surprises 79

22. Momma and the Rules Committee 82

23. Taking Our Show on the Road 86

24. Sunshine Appearance 91

25. Exciting News about My Book! 94

26. Flying the "Friendly" Skies 97

27. *Millie's Book* 101

28. It's a Jungle Out There 105

29. The Donkeys! 113

30. Turtle Trouble 115

31. *Lina Unleashed* Named Indie Winner! 119

32. Fireworks 121

33. Best in Show 131

34. Herding Sheep 134

35. The *Mona Lina* 139

36. My Fourth Birthday 144

37. The Fundraiser 147

38. Paw Post 152

39. Extra, Extra, Read All About It! 154

40. Setting the Bar High 157

41. The Lefse Olympics 160

42. Keeping the Home (Not to be Confused
with the House) Fires Burning 167

43. Holiday Boutique Wrap-Up 170

44. Letter to Santa 173

45. Back in Florida 177

46. The DNA Test 182

47. Aussie or Mutt? The Results Are In! 188

Afterwoof 193

About the Authors 195

FOREWOOF

Hi, readers, Lina here. Welcome to *Sit Stay Pray*, the sequel to my award-winning debut book, *Lina Unleashed*. For those of you wondering if my life with my difficult Momma has calmed down or even if I'm still alive, I have two woofs for you: read on. And by the way, every last word in these books is true. That's why I call my work "Hysterical Nonfiction."

For readers new to my story, I will provide a little background. I am a Toy Australian Shepherd born in Sarasota, Florida. When I was only eight weeks old, Momma showed up at my breeder's doorstep, and the rest is history. I should mention that it was the middle of winter, and she whisked me off to the frozen tundra of Minnesota.

From the start, I could tell that Momma was common sense-challenged and that I would pretty much be raising myself. She tries hard but doesn't know how to care for a dog; she's a hopeless shopaholic; she doesn't know a hashtag from a dog tag; she has almost no social skills; and worst of all—she's a Republican. I can forgive her for almost everything else.

I am now five years old, unless I round down like Momma. Other than that, not much has changed since I last woofed. Every day is an adventure; every day I'm not paws up, a cause for celebration.

Momma continues to provide us with drama and trauma. Like the time she nearly got me arrested for trespassing. And the time she accidentally set our house on fire. And the time she somehow allowed me to interrupt the Republican House majority leader's speech at our house. Actually, that might have been the highlight of my life.

To be honest, we've had some pretty good times, too. *Lina Unleashed* was a 2017 Foreword INDIES Book of the Year award winner, I was named Camper of the Month at Camp Bow Wow, and—best of all—I got to herd sheep on a real farm. Woofda!

Okay, sit for my story. Stay and enjoy. And pray for the little Australian Shepherd.

1

FLIGHT TO FLORIDA

January 2017

Momma and I fled to Florida in late December. It was insanely cold in Minni and Momma decided it was time to escape to the Sunshine State. (Predictably, Momma carped: "I can't wait for global warming to reach Minnesota, Lina!") Although we arrived here in one piece, our voyage was filled with missteps and humiliating moments.

Upon our arrival at MSP Airport, Momma and the cab driver lugged her mountain of luggage to the curbside check-in counter. We couldn't check in, though, because we first had to buy my ticket—something that drove her up the wall—at Special

Services. It was no easy task, but Momma managed to gather up her belongings and roll us (yes, me, too) into the main terminal. Finding Special Services was no easy task either because it had moved. I think we would still be rolling around the terminal if an airport policeman had not taken pity and pointed us in the right direction.

After finishing up with Special Services, we were shuffled over to the regular security lane where we joined another lengthy line. After that hellacious wait and screening process, Momma decided that I should go potty once more and dragged me to the pet relief area.

It was a welcome sight because I *really* had to go! And just in case you're wondering, *this* relief area was in compliance with President Obama's order regarding restrooms: all doggies could use it, no matter their birth or chosen gender identity. I felt better all ready.

When we arrived at the boarding gate, Momma asked some random person if the flight was boarding yet and the random person responded, "Just Priority at this point." Well, Momma thought, *That's us*, and she pulled me into line. Luckily, *just* before she showed her boarding pass to the agent, she saw on the flight screen that the plane was departing for Atlanta. Momma, with a furtive glance around, quietly pulled me away.

When we finally found the Fort Myers gate, we learned the airplane was delayed by an hour. Momma, who had forgotten to bring cash with her, decided that she would use this opportunity to get some from an ATM. Unfortunately, she was not able to access her account because she couldn't remember her password. And guess what—the person Momma complained to at the bank didn't have it either. In fact, he patiently explained that if she keyed in an incorrect password one more time today, she would be permanently locked out of her account. Better to wait until tomorrow and try again, he counseled.

By now, Momma was like a wet noodle and collapsed into a seat in the gate area. And speaking of wet, she knew she should take me to the pet relief area once more, but just couldn't face another interminable terminal-length walk. Instead (go figure!), she asked a man—a total stranger—sitting across from us if she could have some of his water for me. She poured some in my portable cup and I drank like a drunken sailor. As you can imagine, this made for an even more uncomfortable trip.

When boarding started for our plane, Momma pulled me along and pushed her way toward the overhead monitor to see if we had been upgraded. All of a sudden she saw her name on the first class list with the number five by it. Jumping to the wild conclusion that she had been upgraded to seat five (have you ever heard of seat five, by the way?) in first class, she pulled me into line hiss-whispering, "Lina, we've been upgraded!" When we got to the gate agent, however, she gave Momma a stern look and admonished that she was number five on the *waiting list*. Mercifully, she let us board anyway. Happily, no one could see my face.

When we finally reached our assigned seating, we had another fun surprise. Momma discovered that I did not fit under the seat in front of her, an FAA requirement. Just to be sure though, she tried stuffing me in from all different angles before giving up.

Momma was now confused, angry, and a little scared. She was *sure* that she had given the Delta representative the correct size of my carrier on the phone. But what if she measured wrong—would we be forced to get off the plane, *another* unthinkable horror?

Momma realized at this point that her only option was to try and hide me, so she placed the carrier on the floor and stretched her legs over me. Then she unfolded her *Wall Street Journal* and spread it out as wide as she could. Luckily, the harried flight attendants did not see me and off we went.

I just have one question: Is there anyone out there who does not think that Momma should have a (carrier-free) psychiatric service animal?

Lina, Ready to Serve

WOOFDA!

TWEETING: THE NEW BARK?

January 2017

The other day Momma was all a-Twitter. She had heard there was a device available that enabled dogs to tweet. This was exciting news to her. Maybe it would be a new way to raise my profile (in other woofs, exploit me) for marketing purposes. She would buy the device and get me to "tweet" about my blog, and thus increase my readership. It sounded almost too good to be true. Ahem.

Momma did a quick search and found the Puppy Tweets device online. The maker claimed that a human would be able to get tweets from her dog and the device would interact with Twitter.

This was going to be a real breakthrough for us. Now all Momma had to do was set up a Twitter account, and–she quickly realized– she would also be able to get tweets from Trump first-paw!

When the package arrived, Momma eagerly ripped it open. There were photos of dogs asking for sparkling water in their dishes and complaining that it was hard to tweet when one is all paws. ("Apparently, none of them have blogs, Lina," Momma commented drolly.)

The messaging on the box also indicated that Momma could find out what I was doing when she was away and proclaimed "Tweets are the new bark!" Momma couldn't wait to get going on this–she did not want to be left behind the times. It wasn't going to be complicated because the device had only two parts, a tag and a "dongle." She would figure out what a dongle was later.

In her haste to get the ball rolling, she failed to notice that the product had been manufactured in 2010 (that's practically a life-time ago in technology and dog years). She also failed to notice that the tag was recommended for medium and large dogs. Last time I checked, I was still a Toy Aussie who weighed ten pounds.

Setting up the Twitter account was not quite the

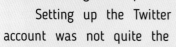

cakewalk Momma thought it would be either. She finally skipped over the time-consuming steps requesting her photo, profile, and interests. Who cared anyway? All she wanted to do was tweet "with" Trump—and me too, presumably.

Next, she focused on getting the dongle hooked up to her account. She carefully plugged it into the back of the computer as instructed. Then she inserted the battery in the tag and clipped it onto my collar.

Not surprisingly, nothing happened.

Not one to give up easily, Momma asked her IT guy, Gregg, if he would help her with an issue she was having on her computer. When he came by, Momma explained that she had purchased a little device that would permit her dog, Lina, to tweet via her computer. She showed him the little pink tag and dongle and informed him that it did not work.

I'm pretty sure I saw Gregg roll his eyes at this point, but he nevertheless delved in. The first issue he found was that the software for the program was missing. When he discovered that there were also no downloading instructions, he called the toy-maker.

After a lengthy conversation, including some questions for Momma about her purchase, the rep explained that Puppy Tweets had been discontinued six years ago (in 2010 to be precise). Turns out, it really *was* too good to be true.

So—much to Momma's dismay—I will not be tweeting anytime soon. Unfortunately, but much to her delight!, Trump will.

@linadogblogger

WOOFDA!

3

RECOVERING: THE CONCUSSION AND THE ELECTION

March 2017

Momma and I have been through a rather ruff patch. She is recovering from a concussion, and I am still recovering from the 2016 election. I'm not sure which is worse. In any case, I have been busy taking care of Momma and trying to get my affairs in order to avoid possible deportation to Australia. Even though I'm not from there, President Trump, the birther, probably thinks I am.

Momma's troubles started when she sustained a concussion in January while having lunch in Naples. Apparently, having lunch there is dangerous. The concussion was serious, and Momma was scared. I did my part by giving her tons of face licks and waking her up every two hours the first night. I'd heard that was important and I happen to be good at it.

Although Momma is better now, she did have some effects from the big bang to her head. For example, she has problems with her memory—nothing new here, but the concussion brought things to a whole new level. It also brought a built-in excuse for Momma's frequent memory lapses: "Oh sorry, I don't remember—I've had a concussion, you know," a refrain I am likely to hear for the rest of my life. Momma even thinks her personality has changed. Because of her weakened condition, I'm not even going to woof a comment.

Not that I'm taking it lightly, but there's also been a silver lining to her injury. Because Momma was unable—in fact, advised—not to use her brain much (again, no comment), she was forced to keep her television viewing to a minimum. Since her programs are pretty much limited to Fox News and its jubilant reporting on Trump's victory, this was a welcome relief to me.

In fact, Momma was told to stay at home and not do much at all. Although there was nothing on God's green earth that she needed, she decided to do some online shopping—just to keep in shape.

The Bose Speaker

One day she ordered a Bose speaker to place in her golf cart. She had decided that she wanted to play music while she golfed like the cool girl with the great personality in her golf league. Actually, I think Momma was also secretly hoping that her new personality would become just like Cool Girl's.

When Momma received her speaker and its corresponding little blue case—she purposely didn't pick pink so Cool Girl wouldn't know Momma was copying her—she couldn't wait to get the music going! Like all things technical or electronic, though, Momma hit a few roadblocks along the way.

For starters, she had to figure out what device would supply the music. At home in Minni she had a CD player with her favorites, but how would she get those "piped in?" (Seriously, Momma?) Then there was her iPhone, but she was sure it did not "contain" any songs except for her ringtone.

Next, Momma thought of her iPawd. She knew that her favorites were on it, but she didn't know if the cord connecting it to her car would fit the Bose speaker. When she got to the car, Momma saw that it wouldn't work because it didn't have the little pointy end to fit the receptacle in the Bose. Oh, well, she would try Amazon—if they didn't have the right cord, it didn't exist.

Bingo. Suddenly it hit her that the speaker might play music *without* a cord! After all, she didn't remember Cool Girl having a stupid cord dangling around her golf cart.

Long story short, Momma finally figured out that she could sync her Bose with her iPhone, which magically *did* contain her favorite songs. "It's all in the clouds these days, Lina," she pronounced, without having any idea what she was talking about.

The Pooch Selfie

When Momma could think of absolutely nothing else to buy for herself, she turned to shopping for me. After ruling out some good devices like PetChatz, a high-tech gadget that *would* allow her to communicate with me in her absence, unlike the stupid Twitter machine, she settled on the Pooch Selfie (for the perfect selfie with your pet!).

I hate to be one to point paws, but I'm sure the only reason she got it was because it was cheap. The Pooch Selfie is a colorful squeak ball that sits in a plastic clamp and attaches to Momma's iPhone. It was advertised to "keep dogs attention" (I know—the *punctuation!*) and would be "fun and easy to use."

When Momma figured out how to use the new gadget, however, she realized that she was meant to be *in* the photo with me. (Did she really think that I could take my own selfie?) She dreaded the thought of a close-up, but she needn't have worried. This blurry mess is as close as we got to "the perfect selfie":

The Academy Awards

Just when I thought things might be getting back to normal—Momma was slowly becoming herself again (I think, although it's hard to tell with the new personality and all), and the hubbub about the election was dying down—the Academy Awards took place. Not that we watched them because that is forbidden at our place. When Momma saw a clip of the mix-up about the Best Picture winner the next morning, however, she pounced! "Good God, Lina!" she cried. "They can't even get the winner right, and they're telling *us* how to vote?" Followed by, "Maybe the Russians did it."

I think she's back.

Lina, Still in La La Land

WOOFDA!

THE BIG REVEAL

March 2017

Momma and I have news. We are publishing a book based on my blog. It will be called *Lina Unleashed*, a sort of "woof-all" about my first two years with her. Even though Momma should have known better than to "unleash" me, she is behind this project. It is her latest scheme to try to make a buck off me.

And that might be hard to do. You see, Momma has decided against sending my manuscript off to the big publishing houses in hopes of having it plucked out of obscurity to become a best seller and make oodles of money. ("We are going to circumnavigate New York, Lina. No stacks of rejection letters for us. They don't know talent when they see it anyway.") No, we are going to make—or lose—money the new-fashioned way—we are going to self-publish. (Translation: the book doesn't have a snowball's chance in hell of being picked up by an agent, so we have no choice but to do it this way.)

The challenge with making money off self-published books is that it costs the budding author an arm and a leg (or "a leg and a leg" as I might put it) to bring the book to fruition. In other woofs, you pay an exorbitant fee to produce it and must sell tons of books just to break even. Nevertheless, Momma has deluded herself into believing that it's worth pursuing. In fact, she already has visions of taking me on Fox News ("The curvy couch, Lina!") to promote *Lina Unleashed* and maybe espouse some of her crazy right-wing views to the hosts and viewers! I, for one, would prefer the *Today* show or *Good Morning America*, but Momma says no—too biased. This from a Fox fan.

Anyway, the book train has left the station and there's no turning back. We have submitted the manuscript and moved on to the design phase. Momma's big suggestion/contribution to the design so far: to put tiny pink paw prints at the beginning of every chapter. That'll make it jump off the shelves, right?

Lina, Indie Author

WOOFDA!

5

THE PHOTO SHOOT

March 2017

Apparently, a book is nothing without an attention-grabbing cover. To that end, Momma took me on a photo shoot the other day to capture the perfect cover photo. I resisted, dreading the thought of posing for countless pictures and the accompanying rigmarole. However, Momma insisted, expertly advising, "The photo on the cover is the key to selling books, Lina."

Momma was quite excited about the shoot, picturing us running through tall grass and wildflowers with wind blowing through our hair/fur and smiles on our sun-dappled faces. I know what you're thinking, and yes, Momma had decided she would be part of the shoot. In fact, most of that morning was taken up with her selecting just the right outfit.

It turns out that I was right to be dubious about the shoot. Rather than taking us to that grassy meadow, the photographer had us meet her at a vacant lot in a rather rundown (who knew?) part of Naples. Upon our arrival, the first thing I noticed was the broken glass and trash, including a discarded tennis shoe, scattered on the edge of the lot. The next thing I noticed was a big red-and-white NO TRESPASSING sign–standing there as plain as day and impossible to miss.

I was apparently the only one who saw it, however, because the photographer and Momma plowed ahead as if we owned the place. At this point, I was sensing that this wasn't going to go well, as you can tell by the look on my face.

What is that old saying—a picture is worth a thousand woofs? After a few preliminary shots of Momma and me, the photographer led us even deeper onto the lot, looking for just the right setting. Having no choice, I followed.

Suddenly, out of the corner of my eye, I saw a man angrily marching toward us. He was carrying a clipboard and wearing a shirt with *Animal Control Services* emblazoned on his back. He shouted that we were trespassing on private property and asked, didn't we see the sign?! (Uh, *yes*.) He further informed them that the dog (me!) was also trespassing and not on a leash and therefore in violation of the law. *I* was the innocent party here—the victim—and now it appeared I was the one in the most trouble. Would I be paw-cuffed? Hauled away in a paddy wagon? Could I get off with probation? Where was Uncle Chuck, Esquire, when I needed him?

Finally, after apologies and explanations (huh?), the officer ordered us off the property: "Just leave right now and no charges will be filed."

Do you see now why I didn't want to do the stupid photo shoot?

As we left the scene of the crime, Momma tried to make light of being busted: "Well, Lina, that was your first brush with the law!" as though it were merely a rite of passage and there would be many more brushes to follow. Nevertheless, Momma was a little rattled herself and practically threw me in the (get-away) car.

After brushing the burrs out of my fur, we motored on to a park to finish the shoot. Which kind of begs the question, doesn't it—why didn't we go there in the first place? In the end, we did get some great photos and Momma, the marketing expert, insisted that I include one on my blog. ("It's called a tease, Lina.")

What can be next—*Lina Unleashed: The Movie*? God help me.

Lina, Perp

WOOFDA!

MORE FUN IN NAPLES

April 2017

I knew Momma was on the road to recovery from her concussion when she announced one morning that she was going shopping. She felt she had been deprived long enough and decided she would go to Naples. [Editor's note: one who is on a budget does not set paw in Naples.] Momma would not be deterred; she was sure she would find something there that she couldn't live without.

The problem was what to do with me. Janice and Natalie, my dog walkers, were not available, and Anne and Gracie, my adoptive family on the island, were out of town. And Momma couldn't leave me home alone for eight hours (*Could* she? I could almost hear her think). It appeared that her only option was to bring me along. She hated the idea because caring for me would cut into her shopping time, but really, what choice did she have?

Momma was practically in a shopping frenzy as she dragged me into the first of her favorite stores. It didn't take me long to realize that this was not for me. I did not like shopping—the chirping women, some who wanted to hold me, and the unfamiliar sights, sounds and smells that overwhelmed me. I just wanted to go home—or at least to a pet store!

Momma, however, had just gotten started. She was on a mission and tried to get me to sit and stay as she frantically pawed her way through the clothes racks. After her beleaguered saleslady carried a pile of soon-to-be-rejected items into the dressing room, Momma pulled me in after her. ("We're both girls, Lina—it's okay. Actually, Lina, these days it would be okay no matter what sex you are," she continued, unable to help herself.) Here I am, waiting for the torture to end:

Momma was loving this and tried on item after item. From time to time the saleslady would pop in and deliver a bit of fake news like, "You look really great in that" and "No, I don't think that outfit is too tight." Right.

Finally, having me in the dressing room became too much of a hassle for Momma, so she decided to make the sales staff part of my village. "I'd like to try this on—would you mind watching Lina for a while?" she would implore. ("They weren't doing much of anything anyway, Lina.")

Here I am being cared for, once again, by others.

The salesladies turned out to be nice and gave me water and treats and lots of attention. One of them crossed the red line with Momma, however, when she handed me a third biscuit.

Just when I thought I could learn to like shopping, Momma whisked me away and we high-tailed it for home.

In case you're wondering—once again, I came home empty-pawed.

Lina, Drawing a Line
in the Sand on
Shopping in Naples

WOOFDA!

7

EVEN MORE FUN IN NAPLES

April 2017

A few days after our shopping trip, Momma returned to Naples to have some routine maintenance done on her car. She had been avoiding it because she doesn't like to spend money on things that she can't bring home in a shopping bag. She knew she couldn't put it off any longer though. The "maintenance required" message on her dashboard had been staring her down for three months now.

Momma had already decided she would not sit and wait for the mechanics to change her oil and whatever else they allegedly do for the astronomical fee they charge. She would ask for a loaner so she could run some errands (code for shopping) in Naples. *This might actually be fun*, she thought—it almost made the pesky stop at the dealership worth it.

Before she could even leave the store, however, a "tire expert" popped into the service area and told her she needed four new tires! Momma was instantly on guard. Here she was, a single female at their mercy, and they might be trying to take advantage of her. Momma couldn't remember, though, if she had *ever* put new tires on her car—except for the one when she accidently slammed into a curb. Not willing to chance a blowout and another possible concussion, she caved. Plus, she wanted to get into that loaner and go to the stores!

Momma was in a hurry—she had at least three stops to make and she needed to be back at the dealership within two hours. That's why she took a shortcut and made an illegal U-turn at one of the busiest intersections in Naples. And it didn't go unnoticed. Soon there was a uniformed officer behind her on a motorcycle lit up like a Christmas tree.

As the officer swaggered over to her car (well, not really *her* car), Momma suddenly felt as though she had wandered onto the set of *Smokey and the Bandit*. The officer, a sergeant (!) with the Collier County Sheriff's Department, was straight from central casting: mirrored aviators, big gut, and hands on his hips (or was it his gun?). He was also hopping mad. For just a moment Momma was scared *she* might end up in paw-cuffs, especially when he demanded to see the car registration. In fact, she began to wonder if orange really *was* the new black.

For once (oh yes, Momma has been stopped before), she didn't argue or smart off to the officer and it worked. More than a little worried, she apologized, and he let her off with a warning. She hustled back to drop off the loaner and get the heck out of Dodge, er . . . *Naples*.

I just have to ask: Does anything good ever happen in Naples?

Lina, Happy to be Under the Radar

WOOFDA!

THE USUAL PRE-TRIP DRAMA

May 2017

Momma and I had just gotten home from Florida when she started to prepare for yet another trip across the pond. This one was to Scotland, the birthplace of golf! She was going with her friend, Donna, and they hoped to play the Old Course at St. Andrews. ("Imagine that, Lina: the history, the majesty, the scenery–the caddies!") Donna and Momma hadn't been picked in the lottery but had a contact who was going to try get them on through the daily ballot.

That plan in place, Momma turned to her usual last-minute shopping and hair and nail appointments. For me, it meant a quick trip with her to Chuck & Don's for dog food ("So at least you won't have that to whine about on your blog"), being dumped off at Camp Bow Wow, and generally fending for myself as Momma scurried about, getting ready for the trip.

In fact, it seems Momma was so busy preparing, practicing and packing that she got a little overwhelmed. One night as we were dragging ourselves to bed, dog-tired after a grueling day of prep, Momma hurriedly set our alarm system. About a half hour later the doorbell rang, but Momma chose to ignore it, thinking it was just her daily delivery from Amazon. I didn't know Amazon delivered after dark, but whatever.

A little while later, our house phone rang. Since that phone rarely rings and it's almost always some Republican group asking for money, she ignored the call. Momma went back to reading her Rick Steves' book on Scotland, and I went back to sleep. It turns out it had been an important phone call.

A few minutes later the back door flew open and the house was filled with an earsplitting siren. Momma, close to a heart attack, flew out of bed, yelling "Who's there?!"

Meanwhile, I cowered on the bed, heart and mind racing. Could this be the raid by ICE I had feared? Was this part of the new Trump roundup plan? Was I being deported to Australia? Was our house not the safe sanctuary I thought it was?

When I saw that the intruders were merely the local police, I breathed a sigh of relief. I'm no legal expert, but I think they are forbidden from asking me if I'm an undocumented immigrant. (Momma: "The term is not undocumented immigrant, Lina, it's illegal alien.")

In any case, it was not me the police had come about. It seems Momma had inadvertently armed the system using our distress code. (Momma, predictably: "It was an innocent mistake, Lina—I've had a concussion, remember?")

A few days later, Momma was off and I was once again placed in the capable hands of my dog sitters, Dr. Becca and Nanny Becky. Dr. Becca brought her dog Winnie with her so I was in good company. And guess what—it wasn't necessary for the cops to storm our house even once when Momma was gone. Here we are helping Dr. Becca at work and waiting for treats:

Lina, Resting Up

WOOFDA!

SCOTLAND

May 2017

Momma and Donna were by now in St. Andrews, gearing up for golf. Happily, their digs were right up the street from the Old Course, a fabulous golf shop and the iconic Dunvegan Bar. Even better, after two failed ballot attempts, their names had been drawn for the Old Course! Beside themselves with excitement, they headed down to check out the course.

Later that day, Uncle Chuck—who was also in St. Andrews with a bunch of buddies for golf that week—invited Donna and Momma to Dunvegan's for a drink. There they celebrated Chuck's birthday and posed for a photo with the guys. You may

notice that Momma has somehow hip-checked her way into sitting next to Minnesota Twins Hall of Famer Rick Aguilera. To Momma, this was almost as exciting as playing the Old Course.

The next day Donna and Momma arrived at the Old Course early so they could practice. Now that the time had come, Momma was nervous, especially about the caddie. What if she didn't play well? Would he allow her to take a mulligan if she ended up in one of those horrendous bunkers? Advise her about dog legs? (Okay—I just made that one up.) *Oh well,* she thought, he had better be nice to her if he wanted any kind of tip at all.

Upon meeting her caddie whose name was Brian, Momma—getting a little bolder now—asked a probing question designed

to elicit information about his golfing experience. In response, he took a swing with one of her clubs using the wrong end. I could get to like this guy.

Momma presumed he was joking, but decided she would take his advice with a grain of sand . . . er, salt. In fact, after a good first hole, Momma grew bolder still and decided maybe she would rely on her own instincts. On the next hole, when Momma wondered out loud whether her putt was downhill as Brian had informed her, he fired back with, "Yes, ma'am, it's been downhill for two hundred years." Momma, who recognized a "dig" when she heard one, blamed him for everything that went wrong for the rest of the round.

After a little too much questioning, second-guessing, and badgering ("Do you want to give me a tip on this putt, Brian, or should I just wing it?"), he took off his vest and started walking off the course. Momma, a little worried by now—would she be the first person to have driven her caddie off the Old Course?—quickly backed off and started to be nicer. (Plus, by now she had decided that he was kinda cute.) She didn't even mention his tip for the next few holes.

Eventually, they arrived at the infamous Hell Bunker on fourteen. Momma claims she was just posing in the big trap, but I'm not buying it.

By the way, Donna and her caddie, Malcolm, got along famously. She treated him with respect, and he in turn gave her golf tips, selected clubs, and cleaned her ball and placed it on the putting surface just so. (All of which Momma was quick to point out to Brian, of course.) Here they are taking turns posing with their caddies on the iconic Swilken Bridge.

Momma says the rest of the trip, including stops in Oban, Mull and Iona Islands, and Edinburgh, was great, but if she returns to Scotland, it'll be to play the Old Course. I better give Brian a heads-up. Fore!

Lina, Still Hoping for a Mulligan in the Game of Life

WOOFDA!

10

THE LAST STRAW

June 2017

You can't make this stuff up. I have now been subject to three horrific events in just a few weeks. You may recall my recent brush with the law when Momma and the photographer brought me onto a vacant lot with a *huge* NO TRESPASSING sign on it in Naples. You may also recall that an animal control officer intervened and focused on me: *I* was trespassing and not on a leash, and *I* was in violation of the law!

Then, back in Minnesota, there was the incident when the police stormed our house after Momma armed our security system with the distress code. That night, the heart-stopping siren rocked our house to its very foundation and likely caused irreparable harm to my little (okay, big) ears.

It seems we were not yet done with the excitement, however.

Momma had returned from Scotland at the end of May, all aglow (key word here—stay with me) about her golfing and sightseeing there. I had experienced a nice, restful time with Dr. Becca and all the comforts one would expect in a stable household. I had my paws crossed for more of the same upon Momma's return. It was not to be.

When Momma got home, one of her first calls was to our landscaper. She said summer was getting on and it was time to get our yard looking shipshape—she loves those nautical terms. In just a few days they came out with a boatload (!) of mulch and weed-killer and various implements including shovels, rakes, blowers and trimmers. When they left, Momma was very pleased. The yard looked good, although maybe a little overdone on the mulch. But at least the weeds were covered.

Everything was going swimmingly (!) until one morning when Momma was making toast in the kitchen and noticed smoke billowing up the side of the house. Alarmed (that term comes up a lot at our house), she ran outside in her nightgown and robe for a closer look. Yup, there was a fire somewhere. Smoke was definitely traveling up the front of our house.

Just at that moment, our lawn-mowing crew was coming up the driveway. Momma, practically hysterical, yelled that our house was on fire. As the mowers ran to the house, Momma raced into the basement, scared that the source of the fire was down there. ("Not my wine cellar, Lina!")

By now the lawn crew had determined that the fire was in the mulch abutting the house and called 911. Momma, realizing that the yard would soon be filled with men in uniform, rushed inside to change. When she came outside in a low-cut top and shorts, the police were already at our door. I, meanwhile, cowered inside the front door, unable to believe that the cops were at our house again.

Soon we heard the wailing siren of the approaching fire truck, and official vehicles filled our cul-de-sac. At what point, I wondered, would we be deemed a public nuisance?

As the firemen, in full firefighting gear, converged upon our house, Momma attempted to explain what had happened. Apparently, the mulch had covered a light fixture, which had overheated and started a fire, she ventured. No, she did not know how long the lightbulb had been on. After a thorough inspection, the firemen determined that the danger was over.

Next, the fire inspector helped Momma turn off the circuit breakers to the landscape lighting so there was *no* chance she could turn the lights on and start the house on fire again. Apparently, it did not take him long to discern that Momma was a walking-talking hazard. Here is the scene as it unfolded at our house:

What can I say? I have reached the end of my leash . . . I mean, rope. These traumatic and terrifying occurrences are getting to be just a little more than I can handle. Therefore, I have decided to take matters into my own paws. What do you think about the following ad?

—Potty Trained
—Light Eater
—Can Fetch and Perform Tricks
—Vaccinated (I Hope)
—Papers in Order (I Hope)
—Good Listener (but Hearing Impaired)
—Experienced Emotional Support Animal
—Comfortable with Officers in Uniform

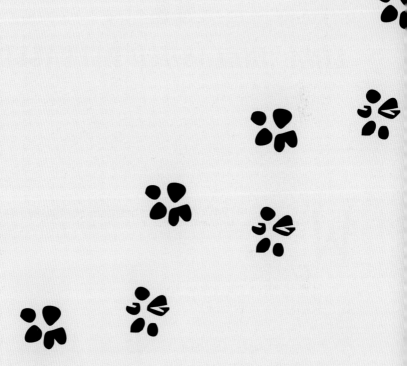

Please let me know if you are interested, but don't tell Momma.

Lina, Rescue (Me) Dog!

WOOFDA!

11

LINA UNLEASHED RELEASED

August 2017

Well, we did it. With Momma's help, *Lina Unleashed* has been published and is available online and at "select" bookstores.

Momma also has grand plans for a book release party and a whirl-wind tour of pawtographings. By the way, it didn't take her long to realize that her bright idea of hav-ing me put paw to ink pad to paper for the signings was a mistake.

Need I woof more?

In addition, Momma is hoping to convince the *Star Tribune* to review my book in their Sunday book section. I am sure that she will not, for once, refer to the paper as the *Red Star* or the *Star & Sickle* when attempting to communicate with the book editor.

Momma, in hard sell mode now, wants me to mention that my book would make a great gift for everyone. ("It is perfect even for those people who aren't big readers with the large print and pictures and all, Lina!") And no more agonizing about what to get for that pesky relative when you've run out of patience, time, and ideas for birthdays and Christmas, she exclaims!

She also asked me to mention—suddenly she is politically correct—that my book is age- and gender- and everything-under-the-sun-appropriate and that there is zero chance that anyone could possibly be offended by its content. She stopped short of claiming the book is sustainable, largely because she has no clue what that means.

And finally, a woof from me. I hope you will give my first book a look. And remember, a portion of the proceeds from *Lina Unleashed* will be donated to the Animal Humane Society.

Lina, Published Author

WOOFDA!!!!!

12

CONTINUING CHAOS

August 2017

S ince nobody took advantage of my "fire" sale, I am continuing to live the dream with Momma. Here's a little update.

No sooner had the fire trucks and police vehicles exited after our last emergency, when Momma decided the house needed a little facelift (incidentally, a word with which she is intimately familiar). Momma thought this would be a quick fix—the contractor would come in and rip out a bunch of dated materials and then put in the new stuff. Maybe it would take a week or two, tops.

That is, unfortunately, not how it worked. We have now been living with a dumpster and porta-potty in front of our house for what seems like an eternity, and there is no end in sight. Every so often, Biffs pulls in our driveway to pump out the potty—or as Momma likes to think of it, "drain the swamp."

We have almost no functioning rooms. Our dining room is totally impassable, piled high as it is with furniture from other rooms. In fact, just getting outside to the deck almost requires a road map. Our living room has no chairs on which to sit and watch Fox News. Not counting the porta-potty, we are down to one small bathroom. Luckily for me, we still have a yard.

Because of the jackhammering and other hazardous activities going on, Momma has severely restricted my movements. ("The last thing we need is a mishap and OSHA meddling in our affairs, Lina.") Here I am hunkering down in my new "safe space":

Despite the chaos, Momma points out that our life could be a lot worse: "At least we are not living *in* the dumpster, Lina." Why am I not comforted by that statement?

Lina, Doggy Displaced

WOOFDA!

13

YAPPY HOUR

August 2017

For the past month, Olympic Hills Golf Club, where Momma spends most of her waking hours, has been working on an event called "Yappy Hour." Momma, recognizing an opportunity when she sees one, quickly inserted herself into the planning process. The premise for Yappy Hour was to host a gathering where members and guests could bring their dogs, have a cocktail or two and socialize. It was a way for people to get to know one another better and meet their friends' dogs that they so often discuss.

Momma, however, viewed it as an opportunity to sell *Lina Unleashed*. Accordingly, she asked the club if she could set up a table from which to run her little operation. She explained that a portion of the proceeds from the book would be going to the Animal Humane Society so it was "all" for a good cause. She would also invite the Animal Humane Society and a Chuck & Don's Pet Food & Supplies store to draw people in and boost sales.

Momma envisioned us sitting on a chair behind a nicely draped table stacked with the books. She would help me pawtograph the books with my little pink paw stamp, while enjoying her muttini and raking in the dough.

Next, Momma's thoughts turned to our attire. Deciding we should have matching outfits, she bought a T-shirt for me ("Lina") and one for herself ("Lina's Momma").

Realizing that she wouldn't have a lot of time for socializing and selling if she had to care for me during the party, she also bought Nanny Becky and Uncle Chuck T-shirts ("Lina's Nanny" and "Lina's Lawyer") and invited them and Chuck's dog, Willie, as well. Considering all the hoopla, is it any wonder that I threw up four times the day before the party and required medical attention?

Ever the publicity hound, Momma then hired a professional photographer—her step-granddaughter, Hannah—to take photos of the participants. As you can see, Momma was often front and center, and Hannah (find her at www.hnsmithphotography.com) did a great job!

Although the event was spectacularly embarrassing for me, what with the T-shirts and entourage and all, it was also kind of fun and a huge success. Let's put our paws together for the staff at Olympic!

Lina, Yappy It's Over

WOOFDA!

14

A PHONE CALL FROM CAMP

August 2017

Soon after the Yappy Hour at Olympic Hills, Momma got a call from Erik, a manager at Camp Bow Wow. At first she thought something was wrong. Had I been expelled? If so, where would she place me when she went off to play golf?

But when Momma heard Erik's news, she was ecstatic! I had been chosen as CBW's Camper of the Month! What did this mean? she wondered. Would there be a ceremony? Could she tie it in with book sales? Or better yet, get some free doggie day care?

Sensing that her imagination was running wild, Erik quickly got things back on track explaining that I would have my picture taken, and an 11x16 print would be posted at CBW. We were to call Patrick, the photographer, to set up the photo shoot.

Did someone say *photo shoot*? Doesn't Momma realize that I am still suffering PTSD (paws traumatic stress disorder) from the last one? Would we be risking arrest again for trespassing or some other crime? Would animal control take me into custody this time?

Brushing aside all concerns from the debacle in Naples, Momma was already thinking about what to wear.

Lina, Camera-Shy

WOOFDA!

15

PHOTO SHOOT: THE SEQUEL

September 2017

I have now endured my second, and hopefully last, photo shoot. Just as I suspected, this one was no more tolerable than the first. Admittedly, we did not commit any crimes, nor were we lectured by animal control, but it was traumatic nonetheless.

Our preparations began in earnest shortly after learning I was Camp Bow Wow's Camper of the Month and would need to have my picture taken for their front lobby. Upon hearing the news, Momma's ears stood up nearly as tall as mine. She proudly proclaimed to everyone who would listen that "Lina has been *chosen* as Camper of the Month!" She was, of course, intimating that my pick as COTM was based on more than a random drawing, such as for Best Behaved or Most Popular or something. I only wonder how many of these Momma stuffed into the jar.

Camper of the Month!
Prize Drawing Entry Form

Winner must be able to attend photo session within 2 weeks of being drawn.

Guardian:_____
Camper (Dog):_____
Phone#:_____
☐ I would like to receive the CBW newsletter
E-mail:_____
We do not share your information with others.

Based on Erik's call, Momma phoned Patrick, the photographer, to set up the shoot. He would take pictures of me and select an 11x16 portrait for CBW for the month of September and gift us a copy. During that phone call, Patrick asked what color I was, and upon Momma's (proud that she knew) response, "Red merle," he suggested that Momma should therefore wear something dark. *Yes!* she thought rapturously. Just as she had hoped, she would be included in the shoot!

The day of our appointment, Momma parsed the thicket of outfits in her closets. She would look best in her blue sweater, but also thought the little polo pony on the front would be distracting. Therefore, she threw in some backups—and matching slacks and shoes just in case. By the time she was finished, it looked like she was leaving on another two-week vacation.

Her wardrobe choices complete, Momma headed to get a blowout at her favorite salon. She proudly told her hairdresser to "Make it all poofy" because she had a photo shoot to do! Fifty-four dollars later, Momma headed home to put the finishing touches on her makeup, and, almost as an afterthought, threw me in the car.

Upon arrival at the studio, Patrick told us that he would first do a series of pictures of me and then of both of us. Although this was not the order Momma preferred, she had little choice but to go along. Welcome to *my* world.

The problem was that—probably because of the Naples fiasco—I didn't want to have my picture taken and I couldn't bring myself to look at the camera. To get my attention, Patrick was forced to use props and toys that crazily snapped, squeaked, rattled, honked, and quacked, followed by a blinding flash of light and a loud pop.

Thinking that Trump had started World War III, I looked around wildly and tried to run away. Momma, however, bound and determined that I would have my picture taken for CBW, kept me in place until Patrick had a few good shots. Recognizing that I was nearly catatonic and worried that I wouldn't cooperate in the photos with her, Momma asked for a small break while I collected myself. (She was pretty sure this was how the real models would phrase it.) Since I didn't spot any bunkers in the vicinity, I headed for the corner and hid behind a giant water dish.

After about five minutes, Patrick informed us that we should continue. Momma took a last look in the mirror, fluffed up her hair, applied some more lip color, and pried me out of the corner.

I, however, had had enough and put my paw down on the entire affair. I scampered back to my hiding spot and waited for Momma to finish up with Patrick. She was beyond crushed that she would not be included in any of the pictures, but she knew when she was licked.

Reluctantly Momma moved on to the photo selection portion of the shoot. She understood how these things worked. ("I'm no dummy, Lina—I know I'll be expected to buy some pictures in addition to the 'free' 11x16.") In fact, she had already decided that she would get a nice one of the two of us, but that was obviously not possible now.

She did have a bewildering number of other options, though: 5x7s, 8x10s, 11x14s and more 11x16s, all in different settings and background colors. There was also a framed grouping of three photos available ("Everyone loves these," Patrick urged). By the time we left, Momma was so stressed over the aborted photo shoot and overwhelmed by choices, she didn't know what she had selected. She did know that she had signed a credit card bill for $375. She couldn't wait to find out how much it would cost to frame her free 11x16.

This is Momma's personal favorite:

And here we are enduring Momma's shameless promotion of me as COTM. All I can woof is two paws up for the great staff at Camp Bow Wow!

Lina, Still Shell-shocked

WOOFDA!

16

THE ANNIKA INTERCOLLEGIATE

September 2017

Momma, apparently forgetting about the pitfalls of working the Ryder Cup, recently volunteered for another golf tournament. This one, the Annika Intercollegiate, was played at Momma's golf club and featured the absolute best female college players in the country, if not the world. Even though she was a little worried about what her job duties might entail, Momma was also excited. She hoped to pick up a pointer or two from these expert golfers. She even hoped to see the legendary Annika Sorenstam in person!

The problem is that Momma does not do well working golf tourneys (lacking comprehension, common sense, and focus, etc.), and she had some *real* responsibilities for this one.

Upon signing in the first day, she was given a two-way radio and instructed to call in on an assigned channel if there were any issues. (*Issues?!* thought Momma, already second-guessing her decision to volunteer.) Then she was to follow a threesome around the course and, via an app on her cell, report their scores to someone or something—Momma had heard it might be the Golf Channel.

This doesn't sound that difficult, but Momma screwed up on the first hole, entering the wrong score for one of the players. When Momma confirmed the scores, and the player in question politely corrected her (Momma now *desperately* hoping she wasn't reporting to the Golf Channel), she keyed in the correction on her phone.

Then, to be doubly sure that the correction was made, she got on the two-way, and after ten minutes of fumbling around with buttons and knobs, established contact with another human being. Unfortunately, the other human being was the owner of her golf club. Now Momma was more than a little worried—would she be replaced as a scorer? Receive a reprimand letter? Be asked to leave the club?

The next day went well except for one teeny-tiny little incident on the third hole. The golfers were on the green preparing to putt when a bee landed on Momma's arm and savagely stung her. Startled, she let out an involuntary scream/cry. ("I couldn't help it, Lina—it hurt!") Luckily no one was in the middle of a putt, but the sting interrupted play and the players and coaches came rushing over to help.

Even though Momma assured the group that she was fine (what she really wanted was to crawl *into* the hole on the third green) everyone sprang into action. The coach from Miami advised Momma that applying mud on a sting has been known to stop the pain and went off to find some. Meanwhile—unbeknownst to Momma—the coach from Southern Cal radioed for medical assistance, and the University of Minnesota Gopher trainer motored out to help. Finally, after a lengthy break in the action and, I'm assuming, a total loss of concentration, the golfers resumed play.

A few holes later, Momma did get to meet Annika, so in her mind the tournament was a rousing success. Knowing her, she's already looking forward to the next one.

Lina, Thinking about an Intervention

WOOFDA!

17

THE BOOK CLUB

October 2017

A week or so after the problematic golf tourney, Momma held a book club meeting at our house. This was notable because she hadn't even *attended* a meeting in over two years. ("Too much like homework, Lina, and I often don't like the book.") This was different, though—Momma finally found a book she liked. It was called *Lina Unleashed*.

To drum up interest, Momma bit the bullet, went to the previous month's meeting, and even read the book! She also brought along copies of *Lina Unleashed*, trying to foist them upon the members. The ladies were understanding about Momma's two-year absence and some donated to the Animal Humane Society, even if they had already purchased my book online.

Momma was quite excited about the meeting at our house. She sent out scads of email reminders advising the ladies that I would be in attendance and pawtographing the book. She even baked what could loosely be called dog bone-shaped cookies for the evening's dessert.

Next, she drafted several questions about the book's meaning, and her friend, Cathy, led the discussion. Predictably, the questions focused on Momma, even though *I* am the author. That was fine with me, though, because when no one was look-ing, I was busy checking out the cookies.

As the evening dragged on, one of the ladies, tired of Momma's thought-provoking questions, interrupted to ask what Momma really wanted to happen with the book. Her honest answer—to have *Lina Unleashed* made into a blockbuster movie with Cameron Diaz playing her—seemed a little farfetched, even to her, so she answered modestly that she wanted the book to be a runaway best seller. (Momma hadn't forgotten that publishing the book had cost a fortune and that it would almost take an act of God for her to even break even, but the *Ladies of the Club* did not need to know that.)

As for me, I'm planning on playing myself.

Lina, Cookie Taste Tester and Aspiring Actress

WOOFDA!

NOT FAKE NEWS

November 2017

I've been quiet lately so you might think things have settled down on the home front. Nothing could be further from the truth. In fact, there are stories that I haven't told because they are *so* predictable and repetitive that you may think they are "fake news." I have concluded, however, that I must not let the current political climate (led by the Tweeter-in-Chief) silence my voice. **Woof!**

The other night, Momma and I were peacefully sleeping the night away when—wait for it—the house alarm went off again. You'd think I was used to it by now, but the mind-blowing noise was as bad as ever, nearly sending me into shock. Nevertheless, I took up my usual "attack" position on the bed, carefully listening (to the extent I still had hearing) for suspicious noises coming from downstairs. Just so you know, I would have gone down to check things out, but the bedroom door was closed.

Meanwhile Momma grabbed her cell and called 911. The duty officer told her to stay on the line and keep the bedroom door closed. He would send a squad right over.

Next, Momma grabbed her trusty "weapon"—a can of wasp spray, guaranteed to "shoot" up to twenty-nine feet—from her nightstand. Next, she informed the officer that it was just her and her little (guard) dog in the house, and that she was armed with a can of wasp spray. She further informed him that she was sorry she hadn't bought a gun as she had planned after completing her concealed carry permit training.

This got the officer's attention and he tersely asked, "There are no guns in the home, are there, ma'am?" "No," Momma replied regretfully, "but I'll be getting one." [Editor's note: "Please, God, no."]

Luckily for all parties involved, the cops quickly arrived and entered the house through a first-floor bathroom door that had blown open. It was an especially windy night, but why the door was not locked, or even firmly closed, will likely never be known. Thankfully, this was just another false alarm.

After a quick search of the house the cops told us the coast was clear. Before leaving, though, they gave me a few sympathetic pets. In fact, I think they may have been sizing me up as a possible police dog.

Lina, Future Police K-9?

WOOFDA!

19

PERPETUAL PATIENT

November 2017

My visits to the vet, and the accompanying drain on Momma's pawketbook, continue unabated. By the way, I bet I know one kind of universal health care Momma could get behind. Just woofin'.

So, anyway, here's the latest. The day before my book signing at Yappy Hour, I threw up a couple of times. Now for most dogs, this would not be a national emergency, but for Momma, it was a crisis. What if I couldn't appear at the signing? Wouldn't she make more money if I were there to attract attention?

The question almost answered itself, so she got on the phone. The vets were all booked, but she finally found one who would see us on an emergency basis for an additional fee of $88. There, I was given a battery of tests and diagnosed with gastroenteritis, a.k.a. an upset stomach. Momma was given a bill for $346.46. Somehow I doubt she made that up in book sales.

A month or two later, I had a couple of accidents on Momma's favorite area rug. This was another huge crisis in her mind, so she hauled me to the vet again. This visit resulted in another break-the-bank series of tests that entailed a urinalysis, blood work, and X-rays. Because the technician was not able to get a good X-ray of my (empty by now) bladder, she told Momma to bring me in the next morning. This meant "holding it" until the clinic opened at 8:30—not easy if your human gives you unlimited water and puts you to bed at 7:00 the night before.

These test results showed that I did not have the suspected UTI, but that I did have crystals in my urine. The tab for the tests and my new "special" dog food? $327.83.

We weren't done yet as it turns out. Along with the bill, the vet also told Momma that my teeth should be cleaned and handed her an estimate of $388.95. Momma was crazed. It didn't cost *her* that much to have *her* teeth cleaned, or filled for that matter! ("And you have such *tiny* teeth, Lina!") Nevertheless, she could see the plaque buildup and reluctantly agreed.

The cleaning took place the next week. Other than the fasting ahead of time, the inability to eat afterward, the lengthy recovery from the anesthetic, and the sore gums, it was a pleasant experience.

There was more. Later that month, Momma went on one of her many trips to Florida and my sitter, Dr. Becca, noticed that I was having trouble going poops. Becca surmised this could be a result of the prescription dog food, and suggested Momma get me re-tested. Thankfully, the crystals were gone and the vet said I could go back to my regular food. The problem was, with all the stuff I'd been on, Momma couldn't remember what it was.

Just when I thought the torture had ended, the vet decided to express my anal glands, just to be extra sure there was no impediment to my pooping! Really, does life get any better than this? As we left, Momma was handed yet another bill for

$137.38. This included a charge for "Cranberry Comfort" powder, which was apparently to—well, actually—I have no idea what it was for and neither does Momma.

Lina, Just Shoot Me Now

WOOFDA!

Pawscript: Mutticare for all!

20

MOMMA WORKS IT

December 2017

So, a woman walks into a bookstore and she hoodwinks the manager into promoting *Lina Unleashed*! No joke. Read on. Today, Momma went to our local Barnes & Noble to buy some conservative audiobook–probably by the likes of Bill O'Reilly–and she noticed the place was virtually crawling with people. Momma quickly realized that she was missing a huge opportunity by failing to have my book featured at the store, especially at Christmastime. As a matter of fact, she had to admit she didn't even know if it was *in* the store.

Forgetting all about her shopping, Momma started looking around for assistance. Luckily, the first employee she spotted turned out to be Brett, the store manager! Momma, on her best behavior now, politely asked him where the doggie books were.

Brett first showed her an endcap called "Dog Tales" (Momma thought "Dog Tails" would have been more clever, but kept her opinion to herself for once), which was brimming with dog books, but not *Lina Unleashed*. Then Brett took her to the much larger dog section of the store, which also did not include my book. When she told him that she was looking for a book that her dog had written, Brett took a guarded look at Momma, but nevertheless said he would look it up.

After a quick search, Brett found *Lina Unleashed* and told Momma that it was in the humor section. Pleased, Momma practically shouted, "Well that makes sense, the book is hilarious!" Brett

walked her over and, sure enough, there were my little pink-and-green books! By the time Momma left the store, they were paw-tographed and sitting in the Dog Tales endcap. ("It's a dog-eat-dog world out there, Lina, you've got to make your own luck!") You go, Momma!

Lina,
Featured Author

WOOFDA!

21

CHRISTMAS SURPRISES

December 2017

Christmas came early for us this year—for Momma, because she got one of her right-wing screeds published by the *Star Tribune*, and for me, because I got my picture in that very same newspaper!

Momma's letter was in response to a "kerfuffle" at Orchestra Hall and a series of letters commenting on said kerfuffle. The principal trumpet of the Minnesota Orchestra, Manny Laureano, had walked off the stage during a performance to protest left-wing comments by guest artist Rufus Wainwright.

Momma was riveted by this controversy. She, herself, was sick of performers bashing Republicans when they should be entertaining the audience. ("Lina, I cannot count the number of times that I have had concerts ruined by liberal rantings.") In fact, Momma had taken to booing loudly or calling venues to get her money back when she was offended. She can be such a snowflake.

But I dogress. If the controversy riveted Momma, the letters criticizing Manny sent her into orbit. Here was this brave and noble and talented musician taking a stand on the issue and being disparaged for it! She, Momma, needed to come to his defense! Accordingly, she began firing off letters to the paper, and on the third try, one was published.

When Momma saw her letter in print, she let out such a blood-curdling scream that I thought the house was on fire again. Luckily, Nanny Becky was at our house and put her hands over my ears.

A few months later, Momma finally got to meet her hero, Manny!

Two days later, Momma opened the Saturday paper to the section on pets. She had submitted my photo several weeks ago for the "Reader Pet of the Week" feature. As she looked down the page, Momma was prepared to fume over the unfairness that her little doggie had, once again, been overlooked by the enemy newspaper.

Imagine her surprise—and the further damage to my ears—when she saw my picture in all its glory in the paper! She couldn't stop squealing (almost crying), "Lina, you are the Pet of the Week!" Unfortunately, Nanny wasn't there, so I had to fend for myself until the outburst subsided.

Lina, All I Want for Christmas Is Earplugs

WOOFDA!

22

MOMMA AND THE RULES COMMITTEE

January 2018

We are happy to be back in Florida and renewing old acquaintances—including with my best furry friend, Gracie! And we do have a bit of news. Momma has somehow wrangled a position on the Rules Committee at her condominium building. Predictably, she thinks it carries a lot more authority and clout than it does. In fact, she is so impressed with her new status that you'd think she had been elected president of the United States. Now that I think about it, how much worse could she be?

Momma takes her job very seriously, and because of her newfound "power," she readily dispenses information and advice that is way beyond the purview of the Rules Committee. For example, when Gracie's mom noted that her fireplace pilot light was off, Momma, with all the expertise of an HVAC technician or a meteorologist, informed her it was because of the hurricane (a tidbit she picked up at a committee meeting). And when Momma took a fall in the condo garage due to a wet floor, she promptly tracked down the head of building maintenance so he could remedy the situation before anyone else fell. She had a heightened responsibility now, did she not?

As with all elected officials, she feels the stress of the burden of the office, too. For example, when she goes to the gym, she uses sanitizing wipes to clean the machines and mats when finished—just in case the building cameras are "trained" on her. She was the one, after all, at a committee meeting who suggested that this rule be added. Wouldn't it just be the bite if she was caught failing to do so herself?

She has also stopped her practice of driving against the directional arrows in the garage, no matter how much time it saves. She no longer brings her wine to the pool in a glass container (that rule, it turns out, was already on the books—who knew!). She is even thinking about abiding by the rule against saving pool chairs with towels.

She also tries to remember to take her trash down in the service elevator. This is not a rule yet, but it's been proposed and what kind of a rule-maker would she be if she didn't set a good example?

There is one proposed rule, however, that Momma refuses to follow. That one, of course, involves me. It seems that some of the residents believe dogs belong on the service, not the front passenger, elevators. Momma is vehemently opposed and has no plans to comply. First, she does not believe that we belong on the elevator with the trash, and second, she likes to use me as a promotional tool for my blog and *Lina Unleashed*. In fact, she had the audacity to argue in a Rules Committee meeting that people *want* me on the passenger elevator.

Anyway, there can be no good outcome if this rule is passed. I am already bracing myself for another visit from animal control.

Lina, Chief of Staff and Stowaway on the Front Elevator

WOOFDA!

23

TAKING OUR SHOW ON THE ROAD

February 2018

I n case you haven't heard, we have another book signing/
pawtographing coming up! Momma is in her usual frenzy
to get attendees so she can peddle *Lina Unleashed*. She has
even taken to calling this event "the latest stop on Lina's world
book tour," as though I were Hillary Clinton promoting *What
Happened*. (Momma on that subject: "That book could have been
two words long, Lina—I lost.") Trying to get the buzz going, she
also refers to my book as a best seller.

Soon after we arrived on Marco Island this year, Momma
set out for the local bookstore, Sunshine Booksellers, *Lina*

Unleashed and marketing materials in hand. She got the usual "Call security" look when she explained to Joan, the manager, that her dog had written a book. Before Joan could even catch her breath, Momma rushed on, saying that she hoped the bookstore would carry my book. Joan agreed to look at it and said she'd be in touch. Momma, wanting to demonstrate that she was part of the Sunshine Booksellers team, bought a cheap paperback on the way out.

Imagine our surprise when the very next day Joan emailed Momma. She said she'd read part of *Lina Unleashed* and would like to have us do a signing! Momma, over the moon, rushed down to the store to iron out the details. By the time she left, Joan had agreed that Momma could do a little presentation, including a reading and Q&A. To create a pawrty atmosphere, Momma promised to serve Unleashed Chardonnay (an idea she got from Uncle Chuck) and dog bone-shaped cookies.

After the excitement wore off, however, Momma began to worry that maybe she had bitten off more that she (or I) could chew. For example, just what does one "do" at a book signing presentation? Since *I* was the author, could she "speak" for me? After all, if she had me speak, it would be a short presentation. ("Woof.")

Momma was also worried on another front. She had promised Joan that she could get at least twenty friends to the event, but she barely knew twenty people in all of Florida. Now she would be forced to scrounge around for attendees.

Using her clout as a member of the prestigious Rules Committee, she talked her building manager into letting her post signs in the mail and work-out rooms. He did draw the line, however, on posting them in the elevators. Apparently, clout as a member of the Rules Committee only goes so far.

Next, Momma dragged me to the other buildings in her complex, where she talked her way past locked doors and begged each manager to post the signs. Meanwhile, I did my best to ingratiate us to the managers by giving face licks. If I do say so myself, I think it did the trick!

Momma also went nowhere without postcard-sized flyers in her pocket. If anyone so much as glanced at me on our walks around the cape, she went into her elevator speech about me, the book, and the pawtographing and gave them a flyer. She perfected that elevator speech in, well, the elevator, where she reminds people daily about the signing.

She also posted a notice on the building's website (doing something of an end-run around the manager) in several categories, even those that have nothing to do with books or pets or items for sale. With this in mind, Momma piped up at the last board meeting and instructed that "everyone should use the website as the go-to place for information on all building events and communications!"

Finally, she brought the ubiquitous postcards to the golf course and handed them out to the ladies at the "wine" portion of Nine & Wine. Here one of the ladies is using it as a coaster:

Momma was not happy.

Her marketing bases covered, Momma then turned to book-signing pawrty prep. The wine had been ordered and delivered weeks ago. I just hope there is some left. Now if Momma could just find someone to bake dog bone-shaped cookies (let's face it—the last ones didn't even resemble dog bones), we'll be set.

Lina, Pawrty Girl & Best-selling Author

WOOFDA!

24

SUNSHINE APPEARANCE

February 2018

A t last, our big day to present *Lina Unleashed* at Sunshine Booksellers had arrived. Apparently, our humiliating peddling of signs from building to building in the fashion of a door-to-door salesman and other strong-leg tactics, paid off. A bunch of people came and we sold twenty-seven copies that day, and a few later to others who even I—a natural herder—couldn't corral for the event.

The day of the signing, we arrived early to set up my sign and put out the Unleashed wine and cookies.

As people dutifully drifted in, Momma was front and center reviewing her notes and props. Kind of last minute, she remembered that *I* was the author of the book and asked her friend Jane to keep me up front so she could introduce me. I think she also wanted her trained support animal by her side.

By now, Momma had gotten quite nervous about her remarks. She had Googled "how to do a book presentation" and had been advised *not* to read them. She had therefore attempted to memorize her "off-the-cuff" talk so she could appear relaxed and witty like Minnesotan author Lorna Landvik.

The problem was that Momma occasionally forgot where she was in her memorized/spontaneous speech, repeating some things and omitting others. She didn't want to leave out her favorite anecdotes, though, so she sprinkled them in, whether or not they fit her narrative. Meanwhile, I deftly worked the crowd, diverting attention from her lapses with face licks.

Sensing restlessness, Momma looked around and noticed shifting in chairs and sideways glances. Sweating by now, she hurried through the rest of her remarks and practically speed-read a passage from my book. When she mercifully brought her presentation to a close, everyone applauded pawlightly and reached for more wine. Am I twenty-one in dog years yet?

Lina, Momma's Fixer

WOOFDA!

25

EXCITING NEWS ABOUT MY BOOK!

March 2018

Yesterday, Momma and I got an email informing us that my first book, *Lina Unleashed,* has been named a 2017 Foreword INDIES Book of the Year Awards Finalist! Momma says yippie! I say I worked like a dog on that book and this makes it all worthwhile! Woofda! We are very proud and want to thank our loyal followers and everyone who bought the book–or may be thinking about it.

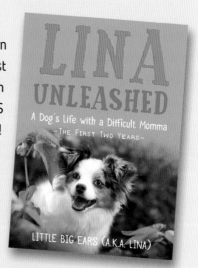

Our publisher, Beaver's Pond Press, issued the following press release on our big news!

March 21, 2018

FOR IMMEDIATE RELEASE

BEAVER'S POND PRESS

952-829-8818

LINA UNLEASHED named 2017 Foreword INDIES Book of the Year Awards Finalist

Edina, Minnesota — Today, Beaver's Pond Press is pleased to announce *Lina Unleashed* has been recognized as a finalist in the 20th annual Foreword INDIES Book of the Year Awards.

As part of its mission to discover, review, and share the best books from university and independent publishers (and authors), independent media company Foreword Magazine, Inc. hosts its annual awards program each year. Finalists represent the best books published in 2017. After more that 2,000 individual titles spread across 65 genres were submitted for consideration, the list of finalists was determined by Foreword's editorial team. Winners will be decided by an expert team of booksellers and librarians—representing Foreword's readership—from across the country.

"Choosing finalists for the INDIES is always the highlight of our year, but the job is very difficult due to the high quality of submissions," said Victoria Sutherland, founder/publisher of *Foreword Reviews.* "Each new book award season proves again how independent publishers are the real innovators in the industry."

"We couldn't be more delighted that *Lina Unleashed* has been chosen as a finalist," said Alicia Ester, managing editor at Beaver's Pond Press. "It's a hilarious book with a one-of-a-kind voice, and it's very deserving of this honor."

Winners in each genre—along with the Editor's Choice Prize winners and Foreword's INDIE Publisher of the Year—will be announced June 15, 2018.

Lina, Finalist!

WOOFDA!

26

FLYING THE "FRIENDLY" SKIES

April 2018

Winter was almost over which meant that Momma and I were in for another bumpy ride home to Minni. If I never see another security line or airplane seat bottom, it will be too soon.

Upon arrival at the terminal in Fort Myers, Momma spotted two men in uniform. They were standing around, doing nothing, and she asked them where Special Services was (so she could buy my "criminally high-priced ticket"). And now that she thought about it, shouldn't I get frequent flyer miles, too?

Obviously annoyed by this interruption of their busy day, one of the uniforms flippantly informed her, "We don't have one of those here—just go over to your airline." After standing in line for ten minutes at the Delta ticket counter, the agent directed her to Special Services! See what I mean about air travel? And don't forget, I'm imprisoned and being wheeled behind her every step of the way.

When we had finally checked in, gone outside for me to potty, and reached the bewildering maze of security lines, we found we had our own lane. *Now we're talking*, Momma thought, *we're in the fast lane!* Turned out, we had just entered the next ring of security hell.

First, TSA told us to wait for a special agent who would walk us through security. He said they had to take extra precautions because police dogs were on site. When he eventually showed up twenty minutes later, he instructed Momma to take off her shoes, jacket, and scarf. I was frankly surprised he didn't ask me to take off my fur coat and collar.

Next, he told Momma to remove me from the carrier and carry me though the metal detector. On the other side, he wanded her hands and informed her that he would have to inspect her bags, too. Momma, normally feisty, was so beaten down that she remained mute (and I remained mutt). We watched in disbelief as the agent took everything out of Momma's purse and tote and looked through every item, including her billfold, wanded them, and held the wand up to a computer screen after each scan. Then he did the same with my little elephant toy. (Momma: "Just like the IRS, TSA is probably profiling Republicans, Lina.")

After what seemed like forever, Momma and I were free to go and raced to catch our plane. She was busy arranging her tote in the overhead bin and me under the seat—luckily she got *that* part right—when a self-important little bully showed up and told her she was in his seat. Not willing to take any guff from anyone by now, Momma showed him her ticket and snarled, "I don't think so." Unfazed, the bully angrily pushed passed us, plopped down, and started scattering his stuff around. Momma now saw that he had usurped *her* space on the center console (this was an almost greater sin that trying to take her seat) and asked him to move his water bottle. Where was she supposed to put her Prosecco, after all?

As you can imagine, it was a long ride home. Considering what's been happening lately, however, I'm just thankful that:

–Momma did not get dragged off the plane;

–we did not have to sit next to a support peacock or squirrel; and

–I didn't end up in the overhead bin—or Japan.

Lina, When Will I Be Free to Move about the Cabin?

WOOFDA!

27

MILLIE'S BOOK

April 2018

The other day I was roaming around, looking for something to do, when I came across Momma watching Barbara Bush's funeral on TV. She was totally engrossed in the service, sometimes laughing, sometimes crying. I could tell this meant a lot to Momma, so without even being asked, I got in the down position and watched it with her.

Now, as many of you know, I'm not a Republican, but by the end of the program, I was a big Bar (as those of us in the know call her) fan. She was the pillar of her family, being fierce and loving. Best of all, though, Bar *loved* books and she *loved* dogs. In fact, her dog, Millie, had written a book in 1990.

Despite my newfound fondness and respect for Bar, I must admit I was a little jealous—and resentful—because I thought *I* was the original dog author. If this was the same type of book (a whip-smart dog telling "tails" on her human and others with amazing wit and charm), I had competition. And look at all the free publicity Millie had just gotten!

Momma was not exactly thrilled about the news either. She knew how difficult it was to get the word out about books. For example, she had been trying like furever to get Dana Perino to give *Lina Unleashed* a shout-out on Fox News's *The Five* by tweeting solicitous comments about her dog, Jasper. It hadn't worked and she was now officially mad at Dana. Maybe I can make a Democrat out of Momma yet.

Anyway, we were curious enough about Millie's book to do some research. After all, we didn't want Millie to get all the glory—or all the sales! Maybe the book wasn't all it was cracked up—or open—to be. In fact, we had both swung into full competitive mode.

First, Momma Googled Millie's book and learned it was called, *Millie's Book.* ("Well, right there, Lina, you have a leg up on her. I don't think you would be an INDIES award finalist if you had simply called your book *Lina's Book.*") Speaking of which, I wonder if *Millie's Book* won any awards. Just woofin'!

Momma knows you can't judge a book by its cover, however, and she did want to read *Millie's Book* to see if it was any good. When Momma learned the price of the book, though, she had second thoughts. The least expensive copy was $59.21. Plus, it was *used*–and probably all dog-eared. (LOL, as you humans would say.) Then she saw that the more expensive copies ranged all the way up to $993.33 and were signed by both Bar and Millie ("With a little fake blue paw print, Lina"). For my part, I wondered why Bar signed the book if Millie was the true author? Did Barbara perhaps collude with her to write the book? Were the Russians involved?

Momma did read about *Millie's Book* on Amazon, though, and learned that it was about Millie brushing legs, as they cleverly put it, with heads of state and royalty. Okay, granted that might be impressive, but could it possibly be more exciting than struggling to stay alive living with Momma? Did Millie have to undergo horrific medical procedures every other day just so Barbara could visit a hunky vet? Did she get dragged (illegally) across the beach to the Gulf of Mexico under cover of night? Almost get arrested for trespassing on a vacant lot in Naples? Speaking of which, did Millie have her own attorney on retainer like I do? I think not. So, you be the judge of which doggie book might be more entertaining.

Just remember–you can still get *Lina Unleashed* for only $16.95! There will be no insanely high upcharge for my pawto-graph. And we are philanthropists, just like the Bushes. Part of the proceeds are donated to the Animal Humane Society!

With my acclaimed first book and working on this sequel:

Lina, Fiercely Defending My Territory

WOOFDA!

IT'S A JUNGLE OUT THERE

June 2018

My world just got a whole lot scarier. I have never seen more wildlife at The Point (as Momma calls our place in Minni) than this year. Is it because we're gone so much that critters think they own the place? Human encroachment on their natural habitat threatening biodiversity and causing proliferation of animals in urban areas? (Momma: "Oh, for God's sake, Lina.")

The Geese!

First, our place is overrun with geese. They're everywhere!

And they honk and growl. I'm not kidding you—Google it. One day I was trying to go potty "out back" (like all good Aussies) by the lake, but the geese were making such a ruckus that Momma took me to the front yard. Guess what?

There were two humongous honkers glaring at us over there as well! They've even been known to station themselves on top of our house.

Momma and I were temporarily cowed, and I imagine *they* will be next, but Momma finally decided she had had enough. ("I will not be held hostage in my own house by some stupid geese, Lina.") Battle-ready, she marched me right down to the lake, pulled the paddleboard into the water, and we hopped on. The usual giant five geese were circling, but Momma charged right into their midst.

As you might expect, the geese took flight—I think they probably recognized a ferocious dog when they saw one. A few days later, Lori, a friend who Momma thinks is always trying to upstage her, calmly paddled by the end of our point and snapped a picture of their nest.

Momma, who wouldn't dream of getting close to a goose nest, retorted smartly, "Oh, yes, I see those every year."

The Foxes!

The geese were the noisiest of our "Big Five" ("Who needs to go on safari, Lina?") but not the most unsettling. That award goes to the foxes. Now I've heard they don't attack little dogs, but what if they're starving? Or sick? Or cornered? Just like Fox News, I don't trust them.

The fox was the first animal we spotted on the lake and in our backyard upon our return from Florida in April. And when you see this picture you'll know why you shouldn't be in Minni in April.

Several weeks later, out of nowhere, one suddenly appeared on our deck. Momma captured a few shots as the fox strolled around for a bit, then jumped down and took a spin around our yard. I must admit, his audacity was discomforting.

The Cat!

We were beginning to feel unsafe everywhere, especially after we saw the *big gray cat from hell* on our deck the next day. Momma tried to act all brave after that when taking me out, but I wasn't fooled. And I didn't seriously think that her yelling "Scram!" to scare off the animals struck terror in their hearts. But what was I going to do—go potty in the house? (Momma: "No comment, Lina.")

The Eagles!

It doesn't end with geese and fox and the big gray cat either. Our resident eagles are back where they are–I'm quite sure–keeping an eagle eye out for me.

The Bear!

Just when we thought it couldn't get any worse, it did. While Momma and I were up at the cabin last weekend, we received a text from Nanny Becky saying that a bear had been spotted just north of our house. Here is a photo from the Burnsville police advisory.

Police advisory?

After this new horrific development, we were a little apprehensive about returning home. In fact, Momma even considered moving, but then had a better idea. This morning she ordered a small hand bell from Amazon "perfect for those that are bedridden or need help." From an attacking bear, perhaps? I feel a lot safer now.

Lina, Point Prey

WOOFDA!

29

THE DONKEYS!

June 2018

It took awhile with Minnesota's late spring, but our dock and boat lift are finally in! Question: How many of you think that Momma actually hired Donkey Docks for their expertise?

She wasn't home when "The Donkeys" came by this year, but her boarding pal, Lori, was at our house (Momma suspected she knew they were coming) and snapped this shot. Momma vows never to leave home again. And I want to be home, too, because Nate—he's the one with the six-pack abs—usually brings his adorable dogs, Leroy and Leila, along to play with me.

Lina, Hee Haw!

WOOFDA!

30

TURTLE TROUBLE

June 2018

I don't know how much more of this wildlife—and Momma's hysteria—I can take. Already this spring we have been terrorized by geese, a fox, eagles, a huge feral cat, and sightings of a giant bear. Last week we had a new visitor—a giant snapping turtle!

The appearance of the turtle itself was not so bad, but as is often the case with us, it turned into quite the debacle. We first saw the turtle in the morning, hunkered down in our backyard. I went over to check it out, but stopped when Momma screamed (The thing was huge! And ugly!) and ordered me to get away. She scooped me up and took me to the front yard so I could go about my business.

Momma was curious if the creature was a snapping turtle, so she trekked out back again—without the little Aussie—and "snapped" a picture.

Then she went back in the house and Googled "turtle with a long spiky tail." Based on her research, she determined it was indeed a snapper and could be dangerous.

Later that day, Momma took me outside for a little play-time. Here I am with my big orange ball heading for the backyard!

By now, Momma's mind was back on her social life, so she had already forgotten about the giant prehistoric creature in our yard. On the way back to our house, she stopped to do a little weeding. Just as she was about to pull a stray weed from a flower bed, Momma realized, to her horror, that her hand was right next to the giant snapper!

Screaming and stumbling backward, Momma toppled over right next to the turtle. I was so terrified by the commotion that I stood frozen in place and watched as she struggled crazily to roll away and get back on her feet.

After having determined that she wasn't missing any dig-its, Momma picked up my ball and led me back to the safety of the house. Momma was quite shaken by her close encounter with the snapper, but it was nothing a glass of wine couldn't solve. As for me, I'm suffering from PTSD (post-turtle stress disorder).

Lina, Still in Shock

WOOFDA!

31

LINA UNLEASHED NAMED INDIE WINNER!

June 15, 2018

On June 15, *Lina Unleashed* was named a Foreword INDIES bronze award winner for 2017! I am tail-waggingly happy and want to personally woof out a big thank-you to the folks at Foreword INDIES! Momma, however, is secretly a little down in the dumps, thinking I deserved gold or silver. She is *so* competitive, whereas I would have been happy with a pawrticipation trophy–that way everyone could be a winner! (Momma: "Woofed like a true Democrat, Lina.")

Here I am with my award. Let the new wave of exploitation, er, marketing begin!

Lina, Acclaimed Author

WOOFDA!

32

FIREWORKS

July 2018

Momma, the rabid Republican and patriot, loves the Fourth of July. And even though she does *not* particularly like having people over ("All the work and small talk, Lina"), every year she bites the bullet and invites friends over to party and watch fireworks.

It should be noted here that these fireworks are fabulous–some of the best in the Twin Cities of Minneapolis and St. Paul. In fact, Momma has *no* problem getting friends to come over as we have perhaps the best view of anyone on the lake. Momma had contemplated charging admission, but dismissed the idea out of paw, because she didn't want to risk celebrating alone.

She also wants the friends around because they provide her with a captive audience for the little fireworks "warm-up" act she and her friend Bill present. They love to sing and play their guitars and require everyone to sing along with their favorite patriotic songs. Occasionally, they'll even let others have the stage for a quick moment to tell a joke or two. This year Momma added a historical quiz to the program and—you guessed it—the winner's prize was a pawtographed copy of *Lina Unleashed*. (This despite the fact that they have all been forced to buy a copy or two, months ago.)

Momma was determined that this year's festivities proceed without a hitch. Naturally, one of the potential issues involved me. Over the years I have grown quite terrified of the Fourth of July noise. This presented a dilemma to Momma, who wanted to be enjoying a glass of wine down by the fire pit, gazing up at the "bombs bursting in air" and hoping no one would bother her. She has not been able to enjoy the fireworks for the past couple of years, however, because she has been stuck in the house soothing me!

This year she had a plan. First, she would give me my Calming Aid tablet early so I would be, well, calm during what resembles a war zone. Then—and this was to be her secret weapon (speaking of wars)—she would wrap me in my new ThunderShirt!

Seriously? Like a shirt and a little herbal pill are going to help when all hell is raining down around me? Needless to woof, it did not do the trick. I was as freaked as ever, and Momma ended up sitting in the basement with me again this year.

However, and this is where things get interesting, it turned out the Fourth wasn't over at the lake after all! Because we had torrential rains that day, the big fireworks show was cancelled and rescheduled for the next Friday evening, two days hence.

Which brings us back to Momma wanting everything to go like clockwork this year. It seems that Rob and Matt, who run the fireworks extravaganza, had approached her a few weeks earlier to ask if she would let them shoot off the big finale from The Point. Momma was over the moon and delusions of grandeur danced in her head. ("Just think, Lina, our place will be featured in the big show!") Still, she didn't want to appear too eager and responded that it would be okay as long as all safety concerns were addressed.

Satisfied that safety would not be a problem, Rob and Matt decided they would indeed do the finale from our place and plans went forward. In fact, Momma walked the property with them and offered her expert opinion on the best places from which to launch and whether the nearby shrubs and trees would be in the way. Seriously?

They also had several conversations via phone and text regarding the details. In fact, she was feeling pretty darn cocky—she was now officially part of "The Fireworks Team" in her mind. Imagine little old her being right in the middle of plans for the big show with hundreds, if not thousands, of neighbors and boaters watching.

She did have one little detail to take care of, though, before the big event—me. She just couldn't have any interruptions during what would likely be the highlight of her life on the lake.

Since she knew that the little pill and jacket did nothing for me, she had dropped me off at the house of friends, Lori and Greg. They gave me treats and took me for a long (quiet) walk.

Meanwhile things were in full swing at the lake. Rob had told her when this plan was first hatched that *no one* would be allowed to walk to the point of our property that night. Momma, thoroughly engaged by now, even sent out an email to her guests instructing them that this whole operation was extremely dangerous and that under no circumstances was anyone allowed to walk to the point.

Late on Friday, Rob told Momma that they had set up the fireworks at two different locations on our property. One was halfway down the point and one at the very end. Things were set and she was tingling with excitement.

When Lori (pictured above) came over that evening, they decided to board across the channel to action central—where most of the show would take place—just to check things out. Momma *was*, after all, an integral part of "The Team," and by this time thought of Lori as her deputy, should she need some assistance.

Rob and Matt were busy setting things up and informed her that everything was a go at her place. Then, to her absolute astonishment, Rob told her that at 9:15 p.m., she was to walk to the point and arm the systems down there. He also explained that the fireworks would go off roughly thirty minutes later. Excited to be given a real job, but terrified—welcome to my world—at the same time, she asked for a little more direction. They showed her a control box (see below), and said all she had to do was turn the key to arm both sets of fireworks.

By now Momma was literally shaking all over, but she was bound and determined to do her duty. She hustled Lori back across the channel.

As though she were in charge of a space shuttle launch, at precisely 9:10 she ordered Lori to accompany her down the point path to arm the fireworks.

Here she is in action (she was especially nervous when she had to step between what looked like sticks of dynamite to get to the control box). I'm just curious: How many of you think this was a good idea? Would you *ever*, in your wildest dreams, have Momma arm something that involved explosives?

Everything finally set, she and Lori raced back to our yard to watch the fireworks. And, by all accounts, it was spectacular. Momma enjoyed the show, but grew impatient for the grand finale at our place. Rob had even texted her that the finale music would be "Battle Hymn of the Republic," the song she had personally chosen.

Finally, the action shifted to our backyard. Mind-blowing fireworks lit up the sky and Momma was overcome with emotion. She imagined that no one would ever forget this night and the grand finale!

She got so excited that she grabbed her phone and ran to the end of the dock to record this historic moment. In her glory now, she continued watching the show when suddenly the fireworks came to an abrupt halt and things got eerily quiet. Thinking at first that this was just a pause in the action for dramatic effect, Momma watched expectantly and held her breath. As the silence continued, though, she knew something was wrong.

Her misgivings were confirmed when her phone lit up with a text from Rob. It read, "No final song. Cops just showed up."

Well, wasn't that just the story of her life, she lamented, crushed. She watched as the boats and crowds looked toward our house, wondering what had just happened. When they finally began to disperse, Momma was close to tears. Now, rather than the epic finale, her place would forever be remembered for the aborted show and raid by the local police.

Luckily for Momma, just as the show ended, Lori and Greg brought her little support dog home, and I gave her some of my famous face licks! By then, however, Momma had already rebounded and exclaimed heartily, "Oh well, Lina, there's always next year." I can't wait.

Lina, Still Soldiering On

WOOFDA!

Pawscript: I swear I did not call the cops.

33

BEST IN SHOW

July 2018

Hi, everyone—I want to give you a quick update on my life before I leave for the cabin "Up North." You remember the cabin, right? The five-hour car trip listening to right-wing talk radio? Yet another lake where I'll be required to swim, kayak and paddleboard? And still no air conditioning, even with global warming getting worse by the minute?

Anyway, here's my news. Last week I started agility training! Momma learned early on that Australian Shepherds are easily bored and need to have a "job" to stimulate their very keen minds. (Okay, I added the "very keen" part.) *No problem,*

Momma thought—she would keep my little body and mind occupied with tricks and training. Almost needless to woof, that didn't happen (she was, after all, busy with socializing and golfing). Luckily my legal counsel, Uncle Chuck, stepped into the breach and suggested that I do some training with his daughter, Sara.

What a find! It turns out that Sara is a certified professional dog trainer and an expert dog handler. Here she is at the Westminster Kennel Club Dog Show at Madison Square Garden with Uncle Chuck's dog, Willie!

Momma was by now all in (she could even envision me on that little table at Westminster) and called to make an appointment. Our first session went great and I loved Sara. She was firm but gentle and patient, and I learned to do the weave poles, the tunnel, and the high jump!

Momma liked her, too, and she bit the bullet and booked another session. Now we're woofin'!

Lina, Future Show Dog

WOOFDA!

34

HERDING SHEEP

August 2018

A couple weeks ago my new trainer, Sara, suggested that I—an Australian Shepherd!—might like to herd sheep! She thought it would be fun for me to test my instincts and see if I'm any good at it. Luckily Momma, always looking for someone (or something) else to entertain me, agreed.

Thus, last week we set out to do some herding at Top Dog Country Club in New Germany, Minnesota. We were both excited as we strolled through the front door of the club for the first time; me, because of all the doggie smells and sights and sounds, and Momma because she discovered the lobby had a shop worthy of Fifth Avenue in New York City. In fact, she was so engrossed in the boots, jewelry, clothing, and lotions that she almost forgot I was with her. By the way, I dread the day—and we all know it is coming—when she asks them to carry *Lina Unleashed*. Here I am on their fancy doggie couch, raring to go!

When I finally reined Momma in, we proceeded to the front desk where we met the owner, Jean, and my herding trainer, Stephanie. Sara was also there observing the goings-on. They were all super nice to me and I licked their faces and allowed them to pet my belly in return. I could tell, though, they were skeptical that I would be able to herd sheep, me being so small and—okay, I'll admit it—a little sheepish myself.

Next, we did the paper-work. Momma reluctantly signed the release of liability form, knowing that she had to or I'd never get to try my paw at herding. The only clause she wasn't worried about stated that she would be liable if I hurt or killed any of the sheep. ("Well, at least that's one expense I'll never have because of you, Lina.")

Once we got the pesky release out of the way, we moved on to the

Herding Instinct Evaluation form. Stephanie (pictured above) explained that I would be judged on my style, bark, respon-siveness, approach, power, eye, and temperament, among other behaviors. After an evaluation of my performance, she would determine if I passed the instinct test.

By now, Momma was getting a little impatient, her atten-tion wandering back to the apparel in the shop by the entrance of Top Dog. Did she need another pair of cowgirl boots? She was also thinking (I can read her mind like a book—as you know), *Can't we just go out to the damned pen and let Lina run after the sheep?*

When the flurry of paperwork was complete and Momma had been assured the sheep would not attack me, Stephanie,

Sara, Momma, and I hoofed it out to the pen. There we found five full-sized sheep huddled in the corner and gazing curiously in our direction. I'm pretty sure they had never seen such a small Aussie before and I'm also pretty sure I heard some of them snicker.

Stephanie hooked me up to a long lead, told Momma to stay put, and brought me into the pen. To be honest, I was a little nervous myself and unsure about my role. After a few romps around the pen with Stephanie, though, my instincts kicked in and I whipped those snickering sheep into shape. You can see clips of me showing them who's boss on my blog at linasdogblog.com/2018/08/10/herding-sheep.

And maybe my favorite picture of all time . . .

Stephanie apparently recognized a winner when she saw one and put a big check mark in the PASSED box on my evaluation form! She also presented me with a Herding Instinct

Certificate from Tucker's Loggie at Lerwick Sheep Farm indicating I had successfully exhibited herding instinct! Woof!

I loved my time at the farm, and we're going back next Monday: me to herd and—my instincts tell me—Momma to shop!

Lina, Farmpaw

WOOFDA!

35

THE *MONA LINA*

August 2018

The other day Momma went to a class called "Paint Your Own Pet." These painting classes, conducted by local artist Maddy Paulsen, are quite popular in the Twin Cities. You should check out her website at www.grayduckart.com.

The fee was $75, which included the opportunity to paint an "original" of a beloved pet, plus wine and snacks. And success was practically guaranteed since the brochure said that no art experience was necessary!

As you can imagine, Momma was all over this. She could already picture herself with a little beret perched jauntily on her head (a la Rembrandt), holding a palette of five colors, leisurely dabbing the canvas with paint as a museum-quality likeness of me emerged—all the while sipping on a glass of crisp white wine!

But back to reality. The ladies were instructed to arrive fifteen minutes early to get their refreshments and to grab a spot at a table. They would have about three hours to complete the pet portrait.

Each table was equipped with five easels, each holding a blank canvas. Each "artist" was given two copies of her pet's picture—one original and one transformed into 2-D shapes to look like a painting. Next, the ladies were given a hunk of charcoal to trace the 2-D image onto the canvas.

The women worked as quickly as possible, knowing they must save ample time for painting. Momma was aware of the time constraints, too, but her tracing took forever and she was rapidly working herself into a state of panic. My image contained about a million lines of tracing and countless amounts of colors—from white to cream to beige to tan to red to brown to black to about Fifty Shades of Grey (did I just woof that?)! Then there were the blue eyes and God-only-knows-what-color nose. Not to even mention the background. *Why, oh, why* didn't she buy a solid white or black dog like some of the other ladies, Momma lamented to herself! She already knew she couldn't finish this painting, even if she had the rest of her life to do it.

When she finally had my image roughly transferred to the canvas, Momma turned to the painting portion of the class. If possible, that part was even worse. She had no idea where to start, so many were the choices. After receiving help–and not for the first time–from Maddy on what to paint first, Momma plunged in.

Although she gave it the old college try, she was quickly overwhelmed by the staggering number of shapes to fill in and shades from which to pick. In full panic mode by now, she gave up on staying within the lines and began wildly slapping the paint on the canvas, almost Pollock-like. She was praying that somehow, miraculously, her painting would resemble a dog when it was finished.

(By the way, it didn't help that some of the women were already packing up. This brought back painful memories for Momma of more studious students turning in their tests when she was only half-done. How could they *possibly* be finished painting already, Momma wondered?)

Realizing she had no choice if she had any hope of saving face (and mine), Momma, once again, asked Maddy for help. Maddy, who could see that my picture was rapidly becoming a disaster—in fact, one of Momma's male "friends" had just walked by and pronounced it a train wreck—took pity and sat down to help. Within minutes and with a few deft strokes, she quickly put Momma back on track. (Okay—let's be honest here—Momma gave her a nice tip and Maddy finished the painting for her.) Thrilled and relieved, Momma gave it a few final touches and called it a night—and *her* work!

Now Momma's friend Lori ("She better remember who brought her to the party, Lina") is threatening to sign Maddy's name at the bottom of my portrait as the true artist. Momma is guarding it like the *Mona Lisa*. In fact, I think it will soon be under glass.

The "artists" and their masterpieces: Jane (Jaelynn), Lori (Sam), Sharon (Charlie), Momma (me), and Vicki (Lucy)!

Lina, Muse

WOOFDA!

36

MY FOURTH BIRTHDAY

August 27, 2018

Against all odds, I made it through another year with Momma and celebrated my fourth birthday yesterday. Nanny Becky gave me a cute card, a delicious birthday cookie, and my very own "Kate Spayed" purse! And because of the extreme weather we've been enduring, Momma gave me a Coolin' Pet Pad. It is supposed to turn instantly cold when filled with water. To be honest, though, I am terrified of the little pad because it is all squishy and reminds me of being on the dreaded lake.

The only bad part of the day was my visit to the vet. I have a sore paw and this was the second trip and the second X-ray in a week. The verdict is out on the cause, but one of my little paw pads is quite swollen and tender to the touch. Yesterday the vet prescribed an antibiotic and an anti-inflammatory/pain-killer drug. Momma is supposed to feed them to me orally via a tiny syringe. Unfortunately, this morning she missed the mark and squirted the antibiotic on my ear. ("They *are* hard to miss, Lina!") I probably won't be better anytime soon.

Here are some photos from my big day!

Lina, A Woman of a Certain Age

WOOFDA!

37

THE FUNDRAISER

August 2018

Recently Momma hosted a fundraiser at our house for Republican Congressman Jason Lewis. Her co-host was former Congressman John Kline, and I was an unofficial co-host as will become clear as you read on. The fundraiser had long been in the works, but the profile of the event was ratcheted up a few notches when the campaign announced that House Majority Leader Kevin McCarthy would be joining us. Momma was quite tickled with this news, but also quite nervous. She *really* needed this event to go off without a hitch.

Among the problems she had to consider was me. At one point, she asked—and Nanny agreed—to take me for the evening. I was doing back flips over that idea. I *love* Nanny and would have done anything to avoid all those Republicans. Unfortunately, though, Momma decided it wouldn't hurt to have me around ("Maybe you'll learn something, Lina") and even found a little patriotic scarf for me to sport. Luckily, it was blue.

The campaign team arrived about thirty minutes before the event was to begin. The group included Congressman Lewis's staff and professional photographer Jana Noonan (www.jana-noonanphotography.com). Predictably, a light (flash) bulb went off in Momma's head the moment she saw Jana, and Momma cajoled her into taking a few photos of us pre-Republican soiree. ("Lina will pawtograph a book for you, Jana!") Apparently, Jana knows how to airbrush, too.

Soon thereafter, two buff men wearing suits, serious expressions, and earpieces showed up and started scoping out the house. When Momma saw them, she almost tripped over me rushing to introduce herself as the host. They eyed us up and down carefully and introduced themselves as the security detail for Majority Leader McCarthy. Apparently satisfied that we were not any kind of threat, although they did take a close second look at me, the police moved on to surveil the rest of the house. As luck would have it, I got to know them a lot better before the evening was over.

The "party" got rolling at about 5:30 and soon the house was bustling with right-wing lunatics . . . er, guests. Since Majority Leader McCarthy was late, they had plenty of time to visit and enjoy the food and wine—and me. At first, Momma let me roam freely, even after the majority leader arrived. She also included me in her official picture with him and Congressman Lewis.

Disclaimer: This photo of me was taken under duress and does not in any way indicate that I support their extreme right-wing agenda.

Just when I got my hopes up that I could stay for the party and scarf down all the food I found on the floor (boy, those R's are *wasteful*–haven't they heard of sustainability?), Momma whisked me off to her bedroom. ("I can't afford to have any disruptions tonight, Lina.")

As you may know, I am pretty much accustomed to being the center of attention, so I was not happy with this turn of events. In fact, I was *so* not happy that I began to whimper. Kind of loudly. Momma ignored me as she had just kicked off the "program" and the esteemed members of Congress were about to pawntificate.

One of Momma's friends, however, did not ignore me. Lori is a real dog lover and decided to give me a little break. First, she took me outside for potty and–Lori was totally thinking of herself here–a little visit with the security police. If I do woof so myself, it didn't take this little Aussie long to "disarm" them! Here I am giving one of them some of my irresistible face licks:

Then, in a teeny-tiny display of bad judgment, Lori decided that I should join the party and turned me loose. By the time Momma saw me I was already heading for the front of the room and Majority Leader McCarthy. "Kevin," as I like to think of him now, took my interruption of his keynote address in stride, but Momma was horrified and furious with Lori.

Well, it turns out that Kevin has an Australian Shepherd, too, and loves dogs! And I must admit that, for an R, he's not half-bad! In fact, by the end of the evening, Momma and he were comparing pictures of me and his dog, Mac, slurping up puppuccinos! Momma was so pleased, she even semi-forgave Lori. And, yes, House Majority Leader McCarthy went home with a pawtographed copy of *Lina Unleashed*.

Lina, Party Crasher!

WOOFDA!

38

PAW POST

September 2018

I have now been doctoring for my sore paw for about three weeks. It is getting better but still needs some TLC (Tender Lina Care). Nobody seems to know what's wrong. Was it injured herding sheep? Chasing my big orange ball? Gripping the paddleboard too hard while hanging twenty? Anyway, I have been taking it easy—no ruff-housing for me lately, although we can't seem to forego the boarding.

Last weekend Momma went out of town and left me in the very capable hands and paws of Dr. Becca and Winnie. Becca administered my meds and Winnie and I played gently together.

By the time they left, I was feeling much better.

Here I am soaking the hurt paw in Epsom salts (not to be confused with having a pawdicure—that would be *so* Momma) with my support dog, Winnie. And today Momma cancelled my re-check with the vet. Something to do with the cost, I assume, so I can only hope and pray that I'm healed.

Lina, Ailing Aussie

WOOFDA!

39

EXTRA, EXTRA,
READ ALL ABOUT IT!

October 2018

Exciting news! Our local paper, the Burnsville *Sun Thisweek*, did a story on Momma and me last week! It's a nice puff piece about our relationship and the writing of linasdog-blog.com and *Lina Unleashed*.

As you can imagine, this didn't happen by accident. Momma had been doggedly trying to get some ink about my 2017 Foreword INDIES Book of the Year award for *Lina Unleashed*, to little or no avail. Never one to give up, though, she finally made a connection with Editor John Gessner and went to work on him. (I won't go into the backstory on how this happened, but what is that old saying–"Everything in life is pawlitics?")

After pestering him with numerous emails and attachments, Mr. Gessner caved and called Momma for an interview. Even though she was quite nervous, she managed to sound coherent and even uttered a quotable phrase or two. When we saw the article in print, especially on the front page, we were ecstatic! The only teensy-weensy "bone" I have to pick is that Momma takes too much credit for her role in the writing of *my* blog and *my* book. I'm just wondering, as the true author, why *I* wasn't interviewed? Perhaps a little protest is in order? ("Spoken like a true Democrat, Lina.")

If you'd like to take a look, go to www.hometownsource.com and search for "Lina Always Gets The Last Word."

By the way, Momma forgot to mention in the interview that part of the proceeds from *Lina Unleashed* go to the Animal Humane Society! I'm always mopping up after her.

Lina, Newsmaker

WOOFDA!

40

SETTING THE BAR HIGH

October 2018

After a brief break, I have resumed my agility training with Sara. And if I do woof so myself, I am killing it. (By the way, Sara has started a new company called Adventure Is Barking! AIB's focus is on training dogs outside of the classroom setting. You can check it out at www.adventureisbarking.com.)

Here I am with AIB founder, Sara, and waiting for Momma on one of our own barking adventures:

For the last two training sessions, we met Sara at Flying Cloud Dog Park in Eden Prairie. One day was rainy and one was sunny, but both were bitterly cold. In case you haven't heard, we had a crazy fall here in Minni with off-the-charts low temps, almost continual rain, some snow, and gale-force winds. In other woofs, a textbook case of climate change if I've ever seen one. ("Maybe you could get a job at CNN, Lina.")

Despite the extreme conditions, the training went well and I enjoyed practicing the weave poles, the bar jump, and the training tunnel. Because this park had equipment that I hadn't used before, we also tried some new stuff like sitting on the paws table and traversing the dog walk and frame, all of which were a bit of a yawn for a quick learner like me. But whatever—I went along with it just to make Sara and Momma happy.

When we were leaving our latest session, Sara informed us that next time we'd go to an indoor park. She said it would be more fun for me because that park has more equipment. Then she added, "And it's all for fun anyway, isn't it, since we're not training Lina to compete."

Woof, what?

Momma and I stared at Sara in disbelief. This was, in fact, exactly what we had in mind. I still had my heart set on that blue ribbon at Westminster, and Momma had hers set on the resultant dog food endorsement, if not a TV show.

Sara immediately noticed the change in our moods. She was already beginning to suspect that Momma did not have the tightest grip on reality and now she was beginning to wonder about me, too. Realizing that she might have a "situation" on her hands, she quickly added, "Or I guess we *could*."

Westminster, here we come!

Lina, Still Aiming High!

WOOFDA!

41

THE LEFSE OLYMPICS

November 2018

Once again this year, Momma and I kicked off the winter season at our home with the annual Crystal Lake Loons (& Lina) Lefse Fest. At its inception, the fest was nothing more than an attempt to crank out a batch of pretty good lefse. Now it has gotten a little out of paw and has become quite the "doing." (This is another term I picked up from Momma. For those of you not from northern Minnesota, a *doing* is another way of saying party or event, but without sounding so fancy.)

The first Lefse Fest was in 2011. Having baked lefse a few times with her own momma, Vi, Momma knew it was as difficult as an Olympic event. In fact, it reminded her of one.

First, the participants must have just the right equipment: the griddle, the rolling pin, the pastry board and cloth, the lefse stick, the cooling towels, and the potato ricer. Then the lefse maker must prepare. This involves reading the instructions (many times), studying the pictures and maybe even watching a YouTube video or two, buying the ingredients, and prepping the dough.

Then there's the actual making of the lefse itself—a Herculean task that requires all the grace and timing of a champion figure skater. And just like any other Olympic sport, to get "good at it" requires years of practice.

The dough must have the perfect consistency and be formed into balls, a little larger than golf ball-size, the recipe instructs; the grill heated to precisely the right temperature; the pastry cloth sprinkled with just the right amount of flour; the rolling pin covered by its own special little sleeve to prevent sticking; the griddle frequently dusted off (kind of like sweeping the ice in the curling event); and finally the large circle of paper-thin lefse lifted delicately off the griddle with a narrow stick and place on a cloth to cool. I have one thing to woof—only a human being would be stupid enough to try this.

So, anyway, back to the Lefse Fest, where all the fun takes place. That first day, in 2011, it was just Momma and her stepdaughter Talla. Oh, and Momma's Brittany Spaniel, Ben. Like me, Ben was excited about the lefse-making, what with the delicious smells and scraps that fall to the floor and all. Here's Ben, by the way. Wasn't he handsome? And he was no dummy either as you will soon find out.

Momma and Talla had studied and shopped and prepped (under Ben's watchful eye) and were finally ready to rock and "roll." And after many grueling hours of trial and error, they finally got the hang of it. In fact, they ended up with a pretty good batch—maybe even podium worthy, Momma thought! Satisfied, they left the lefse cooling on the kitchen counter while they went upstairs to look at some old photos.

The only itsy-bitsy problem was that Ben (wisely) stayed in the kitchen, and when the humans came back, they found he had dragged most of the lefse off the counter and eaten it. You talk about your woofdas! Momma was literally sick—days of working like a dog (ahem!), all for nothing. In fact, she almost cried. To this day, she can still remember the glazed look in Ben's eyes and the saliva running down his chin as he licked his chops. To this day, *I* say, "Score, Ben!"

[Okay, editor's note here: I may not be perfect, but I have *never* done that (I can't reach the counter, but that's beside the point). Anyway, you would think that Momma would appreciate me a little more, wouldn't you?]

So, that was the ignominious beginning of the fest. Amazingly, it survived. In fact, the group soon expanded to include Talla's sister, Tammy, and their daughters, Hannah and Tarra. It also soon expanded to include champagne. And most importantly, it expanded to include me! Here is a picture of us this year, including me with my "trapper hat." Cute, right?

The ladies have become so confident about the lefse-making these days, that it has become almost an afterthought, especially after the champagne. Now they usually post a photo or video of the festivities on Facebook so their friends can see how talented they are and how much fun they're having. This is last year's photo. SKOL!

Next year they are planning on making a "movie" of the fest. Really. With a director and staging and a plot and characters and

everything. In the meantime, here are some pics from behind the
scenes, including outtakes that will never make the cut:

Stay tuned for next year's fest post. I am thinking of calling it "As the Rolling Pin Turns."

Lina, Chief Lefse
Taste Tester

WOOFDA! You Betcha!

42

KEEPING THE HOME (NOT TO BE CONFUSED WITH THE HOUSE) FIRES BURNING

November 22, 2018

Greetings to my furry friends and loyal human readers. I hope you all have a great Thanksgiving with loved ones and all the trimmings. Sadly, Momma has abandoned me this year (take note Uncle Chuck, Esq.) for another trip with her friend Rachel. Luckily, though, Dr. Becca and Winnie are staying with me and we are having a fabulous time. I bet we will even get some turkey! Okay, full disclosure here—Momma does check on me every day and sends hugs to both Winnie and me.

Winnie has become a good friend, and we often assist Dr. Becca at her office. As a reminder, she is an animal chiropractor and her clinic is aptly named Per**pet**ual Motion Animal Chiropractic. We work very hard and only take breaks for treats and potty. I am the patient greeter, and Winnie is Dr. Becca's assistant. Generally, though, we wear many collars—supervising lunch (which can be hard work looking for all those crumbs), helping put up the Christmas tree, and making pets and their humans feel welcome! By the way, there is almost no truth to Momma's assertion to Becca that I plan to unionize Winnie and me.

Here we are by the office Christmas tree and relaxing after a long day:

I don't know how she does it, but Becca even found time to help me with this year's card. Happy Thanksgiving!

Lina, Blessed Bow Wow

WOOFDA!

43

HOLIDAY BOUTIQUE WRAP-UP

December 2018

Well, the dog and pony show, also known as the Holiday Boutique, at Olympic Hills is over for another year. Woofda. Although Momma declared it a big success, I'm not so sure. I'm no banker, but shouldn't we come home with more money in our cash box than we started with? And if things went so well, why did Momma put up a little tent card offering "Lina Face Licks – 10 Cents"? And are Momma's wine purchases really a legitimate business deduction for Little Big Ears, LLC?

Admittedly, we did have some fun seeing old friends and meeting new ones, especially those who gave me pets and tummy rubs. And the Lina notecards did go over well, but I'm sure we have enough left over for Christmas gifts. If you're a family member, count on it.

Once again, I have Nanny Becky to thank for my sanity. She was my saving grace at the boutique—giving me treats and taking me out to go potty while Momma worked the room and socialized. Here I am with Nanny and one of my new friends, Adele:

The night did drag on forever, however, and I was thrilled when we got to leave early. In fact, we left right after the drawing we had for Unleashed Chardonnay. I know I shouldn't be telling tails out of school here, but after giving two bottles away, Momma decided she would keep the third one for herself. ("Too hard to track these people down, Lina.") So, we packed up the wine and everything else and went home. I was dog-tired.

Just in case you still need stocking stuffers, we have a few copies of the award-winning *Lina Unleashed* and some boxes of my notecards still on paw.

Momma wants me to tell you that they are perfect for any occasion from birthdays to graduations to new jobs to encouragement to just plain "thinking of you." She also wants me to tell you if you wish to order some, you can contact us at lina@linasdog-blog.com. She says that we will honor the Holiday Boutique prices of $15 for one box or $25 for two. Tax included. Free shipping.

Play your cards right, and I just might throw in the dog.

Lina, Dealmaker

WOOFDA!

44

LETTER TO SANTA

December 25, 2018

Dear Readers,

Yappy Holidays to my human and furry friends! Thank you for your faithful readership. Each of my posts are paw-crafted with you in mind and it means the world to me when you enjoy them.

This year, for the first time, I wrote a letter to Santa Paws, I mean Claus. Here it is.

Mr. Santa Claus
The North Pole

Dear Santa,

Greetings from just south of you—Minnesota. I'm sure you've heard of our state—one of our towns, International Falls, is known as the "Icebox of the Nation." I bet it's just as cold here as it is at the North Pole! For part of the year I'm forced to go potty in the ice and snow in Minni, where I freeze my little paws and tush off. Admittedly, Momma and I go back to my home state of Florida for part of the winter, but still, you get the (snow) drift.

I am writing to let you know that I have been very good this year. I obey Momma—unless I know better. I clean the kitchen floor whenever a crumb drops. I share my toys with others. I alert her when a governmental official is at the front door so we can hide. I rarely have a potty accident or throw up in the house, and when I do, it's brought on by stress. I don't bark much, and I don't bite or bully. I am a Democrat so I treat all the dogs at Camp Bow Wow with respect and friendship, regardless of their breed or gender identification.

Santa, you will see that most of my list revolves around Momma and her issues. She tries hard to be a good doggie parent, but to be honest, she just doesn't know how. Plus, she seems a little unstable, and we are always on the brink of another embarrassing moment, if not all-out crisis. I hope you can help. Here are my wishes.

For Momma not to make me attend any more Holiday Boutiques. I know she likes to socialize, using me as a tool to make friends and to make some money on my products. However, I'm not sure we come out ahead and I hate these excursions.

For Momma to give up on trying to make me swim. If God had wanted me to dog-paddle, he (or she) would have given me webbed paws.

For Momma not to hold any more Republican funders. Unless House Majority Leader Kevin McCarthy brings his dog, Mac, next time—then it would be okay. By the way, Santa, I hope you leave a nice present for @Leaderofthepack_mac!

For Momma not to help set off any fireworks at our place next summer. This is a great danger to all lake residents and boaters, and hurts my ears.

For Momma not to set off the house alarm on accident. This also hurts my ears.

For Momma not to set the house on fire again—also apparently on accident.

For Momma not to make me trespass again for photo shoots. Like Trump, I do not look good in orange.

So, as you can see, Santa, my requests are reasonable. They won't even take up any room in your sleigh. Thank you for listening.

Hi to your reindeer! I'll leave some treats out for you on Christmas Eve.

Lina

May you have a pawsitively wonderful 2019!

Lina, Thankful & Hopeful

WOOFDA!

45

BACK IN FLORIDA

January 2019

Momma and I flew to Florida the day after Christmas. Momma's step-daughter Talla, took us to the airport which helped reduce our pre-travel stress. Things went smoothly from there, but Momma had her wine and I had my calming tablets—just in case. You can never be too prepared.

The Norgaards

Almost from the minute we got to Marco, we were busy. Crazy busy. Momma's nephew Chris, his wife Jenny, and kids, Adeline and Gunnar, arrived the next day. By the way, here's a fun fact: Adeline's nickname is Lina. Lina was also Momma's grandfather's nickname for her mother. Following me so far? And as one might expect, this led to no small amount of confusion during the Norgaard stay. How did this come about, you might wonder?

It seems when Momma adopted me, she wanted to name me Lina, too, but thought she better get Jenny's approval since Momma's dog and Jenny's daughter would be called the same name. Kinda begs the question, doesn't it—were there no names to pick from that weren't already being used by a family member? (Very "This is my brother, Darryl, and this is my other brother, Darryl," in my mind.) Maybe this should have been a sign of things to come with Momma.

I love having the Norgaards around, but there *is* something about them. Not sure if it's genetic or what, but they sure like to toy with this little Toy Aussie. They often tease me by fake-throwing a ball or withholding treats after coaxing me to perform tricks. They also tease Momma by pretending to give me chocolate or telling her I've just fallen off the balcony. Needless to say, this teasing is not a good idea because Momma is wired enough as it is. Here I am having some "fun" with the other Lina and Gunnar:

I enjoy the Norgaards, though—they take me out to go potty and give me lots of attention. Both Momma and I hated to see them go.

The Solar Plunge

Just before they left, Momma took part in her building's "Solar Plunge."

The Plunge, organized by my good buddy and fellow Dem, Rita, was a huge success this year with more people than ever participating. Actually, though, how challenging can it be to jump in the seventy-five-degree Gulf of Mexico? Momma's on the far left (for once), by the way.

I couldn't participate because dogs are still not allowed on the beach in Marco. If this is not a blatant example of

#doggiediscrimination, I don't know what is. (Momma: "Maybe you should learn to swim before you lodge any complaints, Lina. Just saying.")

Uno

No sooner had we settled in than Momma was on another mission—this one up to Naples. She had recently visited a cutesy gift shop called Uno up there. It was right next to the glitzy restaurants, over-priced clothing stores, and snow-making machines on the street-lights. I know, right? I bet the place is crawling with Republicans.

Jenny and (her daughter) Lina had been with Momma on the previous trip to Uno and saw a doggie book sitting on the front counter called *Living with Humans*. Well, you can imagine Momma's reaction. *Her* dog's book should be the one displayed on that counter!

Jenny, always the diplomat, gently suggested to Momma that she give Bruno, the guy behind the counter, one of my cards. As it turned out, Bruno was the owner and Momma's brain promptly went into overdrive. She told him that her dog had also written a book and asked if she could drop one off for him to look at. Bruno, feeling ambushed if not falsely impris-oned, quickly agreed.

Knowing she should capitalize on this opportunity before Bruno forgot about us, the next day Momma loaded me (her secret weapon) and a bunch of my books in the car, and we headed up to Uno.

And guess what, folks? Bruno and the rest of the staff took an immediate liking to me. Bruno agreed to carry the book and his associate, Jerry, put some on the counter right by the other doggie book! Meanwhile, I passed out face licks and another associate, Kathleen, gave me water and treats.

Momma was overjoyed! This was the "big time" in her book—a prominent display of *Lina Unleashed* in an upscale shop on historic Third Street in Naples. We had arrived.

Before leaving, Momma insisted we pawtograph the books. Then she assured the staff that we would be back in a few days to "check on things." I'm sure they were pleased.

Lina, The New Face of Naples

WOOFDA!

THE DNA TEST

January 2019

T he other day Momma decided that she was finally going to get my DNA tested. She had wanted to do this ever since some folks questioned whether I was a full-blooded Australian Shepherd. In fact, one friend had suggested that, because of my huge ears, maybe I was part Pomeranian or Papillon. Momma rejected the notion that she had paid a king's ransom for a dog that wasn't a purebred, and she hoped to prove them wrong.

After some in-depth research (translation: she ran across an article in *People* magazine), Momma decided on an Embark testing kit. The website stated that the product would provide insight on breed, health, ancestry, and more with a simple cheek swab—a bit of exaggeration if I do woof so myself. That was all Momma needed to know, and she promptly placed her order.

The very next day we received our testing kit in the mail! Momma was excited and read the instructions over and over again. She also watched a couple of online tutorials. She wanted to get this right.

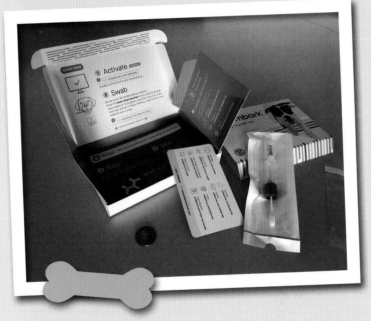

I, on the other paw, was skeptical and dreading what was to come. In fact, it would not be an overstatement to say that I was terrified. I know how things go down for me when Momma gets some new gadget or product. Remember the dog-tweeting device, for example?

Here I am worrying about what's in store for me this time.

Thankfully, Momma didn't perform the test right on the spot because she was busy packing for a weekend getaway with the girls. She didn't want to rush into things and make mistakes. She also knew she might need some help. There is a God.

Luckily, Momma's good friend Lori came over and stayed with me while Momma was away. By the way, Lori and I had our own girlfriends' weekend. We kicked back, played fetch, took fun walks, and had plenty of treats. Lori even came up with a great new nickname for me: Lina Bean!

When Momma got home from her shopping and wining-and-dining extravaganza, she asked Lori if she would stick around for my DNA test swabbing in case she needed some help.

Lori graciously agreed and took some pictures while Momma gave it a go. Knowing that I wouldn't put up with too much poking and prodding, Momma quickly–and clumsily–plunged right in.

As you can see, it didn't take long for me to panic (especially knowing how these Republicans aren't opposed to a little torture) and make a run for it.

After Lori had calmed me down and provided some distraction, Momma was able to get an adequate sample. She hopes. Desperately. After all, the test set her back almost $200. There I am on the left, clinging to Lori after the ordeal.

The next day Momma took my kit to the local post office for mailing. There she might not have been exactly truthful when asked if there was anything liquid or potentially hazardous in the package. After all, she *really* didn't know if that mysterious blue fluid in the test tube was technically a liquid—or if it might be hazardous—did she? Suffice it to woof, the package is now somewhere in the US postal system.

Meanwhile, we are anxiously awaiting our results. Stay tuned—you'll be the first to know!

Lina, Australian Shepherd?

WOOFDA!

47

AUSSIE OR MUTT?
THE RESULTS ARE IN!

February 2019

Yesterday, we received the results of my DNA test from Embark. Momma and I were quivering with excitement and curiosity. Although the results also covered health and ancestry, we were mostly curious about my breed. Would I be a purebred or a hybrid? She was hoping I was all Aussie, but I didn't care. As with humans, I am a big proponent of doggie diversity. (Momma: "Whatever.") Anyway, here goes!

My Health

The health section of the report covered diseases for which I may be at risk, a carrier, or clear. First, I am thrilled to report that I did not test positive for any of the "at risk" diseases screened for.

Next, I learned I am a "carrier" for only one, a recessive genetic trait called progressive retinal atrophy. Luckily, I will not suffer any symptoms, but must be mindful of the gene if I "should have children." Apparently, Embark recognizes that I'm almost human.

Finally, I tested "clear" for eight diseases common to my breed and "clear" of the 163 others included in the test.

Yay! All great news! Doesn't this just beg the question, though—why am I always at the vet?

My Breed

And then, the result we'd been waiting for. What am I really? This may come as no surprise, with my sheep-herding skills and all, but the tests confirmed that I am 100 percent Miniature Australian Shepherd! (Embark's test results do not differentiate between minis and toys.) And *this* is their description of my breed: "Miniature American Shepherds have the trainability, intelligence, and energy of the larger Aussie cousins, and excel at outdoors activities and agility competitions."

Well, I couldn't have woofed it better myself. So far, I'd give Embark an A+ on their work.

My maternal ancestors can be traced back to South Asia (looks like China according to the map) and Europe. Dogs with which I have genetic commonality include English Setters, English Bulldogs, and American Eskimo Dogs.

My paternal ancestors cannot be traced because I do not have the Y chromosome (girls have XX makeup) necessary for that research. And speaking of chromosomes, did you know dogs have thirty-eight, while humans have only twenty-three? Sounds to me like we might be a tad superior to our human companions, after all.

And here's the most interesting thing of all about my genetics: my makeup includes 1.8 percent "wolfiness." This is considered high as most dogs score 1 percent or less on the wolfy scale! This does not mean that my recent ancestors are wolves, but that I carry ancient wolf genes that go back thousands of years. Embark ends its summary by noting the genes "are bits of a wild past that survive in your dog." Maybe I really am my Momma's daughter.

Here I am with my Valentine's Day gift from her. Looking a little wolfy, don't you think?

My test results also predicted that my adult weight will be twenty-five pounds, and that I am currently thirty-nine years old (one of Momma's past fake ages). Ex*cuse* me. First, I weigh eleven and one-half pounds, and Momma will *never* let me get to twenty-five—even if she has to limit me to one morsel of food per day for the rest of my life. And second, I know I have the maturity of a thirty-nine-year-old, but if that age is accurate chronologically, I'll be older than Moses when I die. May have to lower that grade to an A-!

My Relatives/Ancestry

This was a bit of a disappointment as I expected a family tree showing my grandparents, parents, siblings, aunts, uncles, and cousins. Instead, all I learned was that (in addition to some more distant relatives) I share 39 percent of my DNA makeup with an Aussie named Bandit. Frankly, this Bandit is kind of cute. The site says he has been a member of Embark since February 15, 2018. Actually, this sounds a bit like online dating, doesn't it? I'm going to drop him a line. Momma, are you paying attention?

In closing, I'm going to share a couple of doggie fun facts from Embark: Compared to humans, we have twice the amount of muscles in our ears and hearing that goes four times the distance, but only one-fifth of the taste buds.

Lina, Pure Aussie

WOOFDA!

AFTERWOOF

Once again, I want to thank Momma for doing her best to raise and care for me. I still think she may be trainable.

And big-time thanks to the rest of my "village" for continuing to provide me with safe space. First, to my Nanny Becky for always having my back. Also, to my Minnesota sitter, Dr. Becca (Per**pet**ual Motion Animal Chiropractic); my Florida dog walkers, Janice and Natalie (Nanny Paws Pet Sitting Services); and Momma's friend Lori, who sits with me occasionally in both states.

I also want to give a big woof-out to the Animal Humane Society and Helping Paws of Minnesota. They are the best! AHS cares for roughly 23,000 animals every year and provides innovative leadership in shelter care and animal medical and behavioral programs. In short, they make the world a more humane place for our furry friends.

Helping Paws of Minnesota breeds, trains, and places service dogs for people with physical disabilities and veterans and first responders with PTSD.

Proceeds from this book will be donated to these two worthy organizations. If you are so moved, you can also contribute to them at www.animalhumanesociety.com or helpingpaws.org.

I hope *Sit Stay Pray* brought a smile to your face. Or maybe even a belly laugh. That is always my goal. Working on this book was a labor of love for both Momma and me, and we thank you for your loyal readership. And remember, you can continue to follow our adventures at linasdogblog.com.

Lina, Humorist and Humanitarian

WOOFDA!

ABOUT THE AUTHORS

Lina is a five-year-old Toy Australian Shepherd who hails from Florida. She is an acclaimed author, blogger, and keen observer of human behavior.

When Lina is not busy writing, she enjoys chasing her big orange ball, performing tricks, and playing with her furry friends. She does not enjoy being in any lake, river, stream, ocean, the rain or even wet grass. Unfortunately for Lina, she and her human, Robin Kelleher, divide their time between Minnesota, Land of 10,000 Lakes, and Marco Island, one of the Ten Thousand Islands of Florida.

Lina's momma and co-author, a Minnesota native, is a labor and employment law attorney, but her interests are wide and varied. She was formerly a music teacher and realtor. She loves to golf, paddleboard, read, write, travel, and tend to her herb garden. She also tends to Lina who tends to think her momma is a little ditzy.